The Incomplete Explanation

By

Mark Praakel

ISBN: 1-4033-5550-9 (e-book)
ISBN: 1-4033-5551-7 (Paperback)

This book is printed on acid free paper.

1stBooks – rev. 09/11/02

With a revolting panic, Elinore remembers that she has forgotten her wallet at home. Her fear alone tells her that she cannot possibly pay for the meal that she and her best friend Yasmine have indecently devoured over the past half hour to forty-five minutes.

Elinore buys some time by pretending that nothing is wrong and cleverly invites Yasmine into a spiralling, open-ended conversation about her favourite topic- her son Harold. The stall tactic coyly allows her to plan the next move.

It is as sticky a situation to be in as she has ever been; that is being trapped in a binding verbal contract to pay for the meal that the two old friends could clearly not afford considering Elinore's unfortunate cash flow circumstance.

"So Yasmine, has Ronald decided what to do next year after he finishes high school?"

Before Yasmine can even begin the long-winded future expectations of her perfect little angel Elinore slips into her subconscious thoughts. She traces her steps back from the embarrassing affair to a time much earlier in the night. Good form expects that there be an attempt to uncover the anonymity of the exact moment when she mislaid her wallet. Her own pride dictates a need to find an adequate, respectable end to her misery.

After all, the two of them have been sitting at the table sipping coffee after dinner for who knows how long. People must be starting to notice. It would not be easy to explain her mishap let alone deal with the prejudicial glares of the unforgiving waitress.

As she plays back the day in her mind Elinore recalls an episode of mild disgust for her husband. Not the type of disgust that comes from outright hatred but rather the disgust that one feels when a build up of anxiety mixes with repetitive nagging.

A mess of scattered magazines. Her inconsiderate husband left a mess of scattered magazines out for all to see. The very same magazines that she asked be gathered beneath the end table visually out of sight but which are instead spread carelessly on top of the coffee table. She delivers a subtle shake of her head before continuing.

As vividly as if it were yesterday she recalls putting her wallet down on the edge of her couch at home thereby freeing up both hands to move his mess under the end table beside the couch.

With a jerk, she is thrown back into the reality of her dilemma. Leaving Yasmine at the table to defend the cheque presumably by herself she leaps to her feet. Up quickly and out the door only to be startled by the probing rays of the sun now unveiling itself from behind a storm cloud.

Elinore covers her eyes and starts walking with a quickened pace towards her car. She walks around almost aimlessly and twirls a couple of times in an attempt to orient herself. Her delusional confusion is enhanced by the brow beating sun. Elinore stops under the cool shade of the giant oak tree to catch her breath.

After wiping her forehead ever so eloquently her focus is drawn to the innocence of youth that she associates with a pair of initials carved into the mighty oak. The initials are engulfed in a giant heart.

She starts to feel sad. At closer inspection it becomes evident that the feelings did not last. Someone defaced the love. A scar is left in the bark of the frail tree. It is scabbed where one set of the initials has been chopped out. It reads, "XXX loves Wanda forever". Sometimes forever ends before we want it to end. Elinore knows what it is like to have time run out on forever.

She admires the sentiment for more than a moment but is drawn back into her problem. Turning once more, she is thrown by the reflection of the moon off a nearby brook. With remarkable care she scales down the low-grade ditch to the water and pops off her shoes. The task is made more difficult by Elinore's slowly moving pupils in the approaching darkness.

The cool water of the brook is refreshing but she of course raises her slacks to avoid getting them wet. The night wind chills her bare legs. A deep, filling breath as she trots across the shallow brook. The scent is not exactly what she expects but it certainly is not disappointing.

Now facing an obstacle that she has not faced since she was a very young girl back in England, Elinore approaches a twisted wire fence. The fence is old and decrepit. Time has not been good to it either. She wonders if it ever was a sturdy fence or if the fate of the fence was always to be less than adequate.

With the enthusiasm of a boy on his first day at camp she tosses her thirty-nine year old frame over the fence and lands on both feet simultaneously. Pleased with herself she is shocked to see that the rickety old fence has left her physically wounded. The piercing of her skin scares her. The second finger on her left hand is now bleeding like a sieve and the pain will eventually come. Elinore certainly has enough experience to know.

As she walks up to her house she licks the blood away and shakes her finger almost dismissing the wound completely. It is just another battle scar from a bitter, old foe. She raises her eyebrow justifying a question to herself.

Funny as it sounds, Elinore cannot definitively recognize her own backyard even though she knows that it is her house. It is the same house in which she and her husband have been living for the past seven years. After some thought the explanation becomes clear.

The logical explanation is that she does not recognize the house because they do not have a barbecue. Like so many other people without barbecues across the land they never have reason to use their backyard. It is truly a shame because it really is a lovely setting.

Elinore steps up to the back and opens the door. It enters directly into her kitchen. She takes a quick peek at the sink like she always does and is pleased to see that the dishes are all done and that the dish towel is hanging properly in front of the stove.

Her face illuminates when she sees Valentine, a beautiful black Labrador with a shiny coat- *her* beautiful black Labrador, with a shiny coat. Valentine boasts having been sired by top rated, pure bread canines. Elinore fights back the urge to become visibly moved. She has not seen Valentine since he was hit by a roaring performance automobile in Hull, England.

The loyal beast wags his tale and politely asks her to shut the door since the cool night wind is disturbing his sleep. With the unsound logic of an infant she obliges him but spins around quickly in amazement. The double take is severed short by something even more alarming.

Her inability to challenge what has just happened is due to her fascination with the pure, white pigeon that has perched itself on her four-slice toaster. The very same bird begins to chirp in a high pitched melody.

Elinore never really liked *that* toaster. In fact she hates it. She can only make four slices of toast with it. There is only one prong on the toaster. Most definitely it is a flaw in the basic design. Even if she only wants two pieces of toast, four slices have to be cooked. The single prong makes it so that all sections of the toaster are lowered at the same time into the cooking section of the appliance. If she decided to cook only two slices she would have two slices cooking while the empty slots would heat up pointlessly.

Chirp! She turns her focus again. Chirp! Her eyes stare at the pigeon. Chirp!

She tries harder to focus. The irony of the situation is that the more Elinore focuses on the pigeon the more difficult it becomes to see, though that is not real irony.

Chirp! Elinore can feel her eyes pulling to open. Chirp! She breathes a little deeper. Chirp! Everything turns a rich shade of black. She finds herself immersed in blackness. Her heart jumps. The aged should never indulge in utter chaos.

Elinore strains to redeploy her vision. On account of her slower pupil speed Elinore's efforts seem much more fatiguing.

There are some figures in the darkness. Not the white pigeon. Red figures. Much smaller. Her eyes are no help. She raises her head and exaggerates the extent to which her eyes are open. Finally, the red figures form into their proper shapes. As she reads them in disgust she throws her head back down appreciating that she has indeed fooled herself again.

This is not the first fight of this kind that she has had. Elinore is the type of woman who finds it important to fool herself in order to get up on time. The guise of the alarm taking the form of an innocent pigeon is refreshing. Most times it is a fire alarm. The fire alarm tends to frighten her.

Like a lot of people, Elinore lacks morning time enthusiasm. Hearing the alarm can actually cause her anxiety. It takes more to get her up in the mornings and she has adapted to this over time.

Years ago she noticed that if her alarm was set to a round number she would sleep right through it. Her alarm would go off and she would awaken from a terrible dream. A quick glance at the clock was all she required to again orient herself to the time of the day. It was easy. Seven o'clock was a simple seven followed by two zeros. It made sense. It did not take a lot of effort and she could reduce her tension about the impending danger knowing that it was only a dream. Her head would lie back down and again she was asleep.

Elinore finds that if she changes the time at which her alarm goes off she forces herself to pay more attention. The numbers are not necessarily as systematic. Six, followed by a five then an eight may only be two minutes shy of seven o'clock but can mean a world of difference.

By the time she can focus properly on her alarm clock Elinore is that one vital step closer to being up and about. Some days when she wakes to her alarm it is not about the digits themselves. She may awaken the next day to six, five, and seven.

A seven instead of an eight. One minute. A minute that may mean the difference between sleeping in or getting up; that may mean making a traffic light instead of being stuck in traffic; or that may mean avoiding a terrible accident. Time governs us for most of our existence. How often does one extend a thought to the importance of a minute? If Elinore thinks about this argument, a single minute can scare her even more than the fire alarm. Nobody can genuinely sleep while they are thinking.

Once the frustration alleviates itself and Elinore again finds the strength to endure another day she gently lifts the covers and crawls out of bed. She does so in a manor that will not awaken her husband who enjoys his extra thirty minutes of sleep like a convicted felon enjoys his last meal.

Elinore fondles and feels her way to the dresser and grabs the clothes that she has laid out the night before then heads for the bathroom. As she enters, she consciously closes the door behind her before turning on the light so that her husband's rest is not disturbed.

She dresses in front of the mirror and it is easy to see that she is not a morning person. Her blond hair is frazzled and looks nothing like the hair of the woman on the box from which it came.

The day is typical. The curious aspect is that Elinore wonders if it is a typical day. Such a day would work well for her. Typical is a good way to describe Elinore. She has average features in most respects. Her eyes are average, her lips are average and her physique is what you would expect from a thirty-nine year old English woman. Even her nose is average. Not too big but definitely not too small.

Over all her appearance would not turn any heads. It would be apparent, however, to anyone who really looked that in her day she would catch the attention of many men.

Elinore showers at night so her morning routine dictates that she merely freshen up and get dressed. When she is finished she goes downstairs and has a bite to eat before going to work. It is a typical start to a day that may turn out to be anything but ordinary.

Elinore enters the kitchen and is instinctively stricken with an unexpected task. Today is the first of the month so she stops for a second to turn over the calendar page.

A smile fills her face as she is pleased by a picture of two kittens who have decided to spend their time playing with what seems to be an extra role of toilet paper. Elinore laughs almost out loud and shakes her head as she walks deeper into the kitchen to start her breakfast.

As always, the first deed is a faint glance to the sink to check the status of the dishes. Not missing a step she plugs in the kettle first lifting it to make sure that there is enough water for her morning cup of tea. Experience again takes over. Routine is the offspring of both time and failure.

Elinore calmly advances to the refrigerator and takes out four pieces of bread from the bag making sure that the four slices are of equal size. This means that she bypasses the end slices to choose from the middle of the loaf. Everyone knows that she could never finish off all four pieces but of course the toaster commands that four be cooked.

As she puts the slices of bread into the slots her thoughts alter to decide on what type of topping to use. The task would normally not take so long except that it is early morning and her brain is still struggling to wake. Her decision is on blueberry jam so she shuffles over to the refrigerator again and seizes the jam container as well as some milk for her tea.

While still in a state of bewilderment Elinore retrieves a tea bag from a box in the cupboard and places it in her cup covering it generously with milk. She puts the milk back into the refrigerator and as she does so the water in the kettle begins to boil. Like a seasoned veteran of breakfast she hurries back to pull the cord. Her entire body quakes with terror as the toast in the unwanted piece of equipment pops up with enthusiasm.

In a hurry Elinore pours the water and replaces the kettle. She attempts to speed things along by grabbing for a spoon and a plate at the same time but cannot complete either task simultaneously. Realizing her unsuccessful attempt she turns all of her attention to the plate and places it on the counter. It is then that she reaches to get a spoon for her tea and a knife to spread the jam.

With her left hand Elinore stirs the tea bag around the cup. She does not look at her finger but remembers her injury from the dream. After a moment she takes the toast from the toaster with her right hand.

The tea bag floats to the top and she scoops it out with the spoon, dispensing it into the garbage immediately. The tea is not very steep for an early morning jolt of rejuvenescence.

With the skill of a tradesman Elinore carves out enough jam for two of the four slices of toast, spreads the topping on generously and proceeds to nibble at them bit by bit. She washes her fourth and fifth bite down with a large gulp of tea and checks her watch for the time, out of habit.

Everything is going according to schedule so she finishes off her meal and slips her shoes on at a comfortable pace. There is a problem that needs to be addressed before she can leave. Elinore opens her change purse and notices that she will need an extra dollar fifteen to make it to and from her work by bus.

A troubled expression obstructs her face as she recalls a time not long ago when her whole trip would have cost *that* amount with enough left over to buy a small candied treat. The slender silhouette delicately walks past the desk by the front door and pilfers the money from her husband's wallet. She justifies her action without words. A simple nod of her head.

The unwritten contract to which Elinore and her husband agreed is for Elinore's husband to take their car since she is only a five or ten minute bus ride to work. He, on the other hand, must drive a good forty to forty-five minutes to his office. In her mind she figures that because he is awarded the convenience of their automobile then he can suffer the financial constraint of her bus ride.

She gathers up the necessary fare for the ride into work and separates it from the money needed for the ride home. The latter portion is placed into her change purse and the former is transferred directly into her right pocket, keeping it at hand.

The simple task has cognitive roots. Elinore needs to know that the money will be in her right pocket so it has become the only pocket she uses. She has negated the use of any other pocket. Time again has shown her that using more pockets merely increases the number of places that one has to look when searching for something. This does limit the number of things that one can carry. Elinore is both fully aware and comfortable with the limitation. The truth is that there can be no convenience without sacrifice. If Elinore wants to find something that she has brought with her she knows that the item will be either in her right pant pocket, her left jacket pocket or in the zippered compartment of her change purse.

Having collected her materials she takes another long look to ensure that she has not forgotten anything and whisks out the door thoughtlessly slamming it shut behind her.

That is what a typical morning looks like in the life of Elinore. It does not seem to be drastically different from the morning of many people. So what makes Elinore any different from the average person, putting aside that bizarre idiosyncrasy with her alarm clock?

Being typical does not mean that Elinore has no identity of her own. It is just that in most respects she does not stand out in any particular way.

What we do is a snap shot of the people that we are. The way that we accomplish even the most menial tasks delves into both our personalities and our pasts. We learn from our experiences and we learn from those who affect us so we all characteristically learn the same things. The same lessons and the same basic morale structures. We learn these lessons, however, in different fashions and at different times in our lives.

Is it a learned condition to complete simple tasks in a socially accepted fashion?

It would be difficult to imagine that Elinore is unlike many people. Some feel that they themselves are typical. Everyone knows someone who is. Without sighting specifics it is not easy to find many people who are not typical. There is a reason that we use the term "average".

When the common reactions that the majority of people will give are socially accepted there is behaviourally nothing setting people apart. We judge people by the contrast between what they do and our perception of what they might have done. Though, to really know people we need to understand *why* they had to react the way that they did.

"Average" implies a perceived willingness in an individual to act similarly to a majority of people in common situations. When we think about a typical person their actions and their personality traits always resemble normal social actions and interactions. There is nothing that is supposed to jump out of the average.

Every child, for example, has his or her own individuality. Each child needs the same things from his or her parents and from the other people around him or her. Children act and react to ensure that they get these things. They react differently and at different times but the bottom line is that they test. Every child tests.

How we relate and react to the testing varies and can have very drastic ranges. Children progress and develop skills by mimicking others. As they age and develop, these skills naturally aid in comparing them with other people who also have either the exact same or similar skills.

Eventually we will all feel trapped by being average. It is only the skills that we have acquired that seem greater comparably to what most people possess that will set us apart. How does one excel above a group to which he or she does not belong?

When altering ourselves to be unique we must pass through the stage of being similar. No matter how confident we are we strive to attain similarity before we strive to be unique.

Personality traits on the other hand are innate in all human individuals. The differences lay in the varying degree to which each individual allows each personality trait to expand or grow. We all have the ability to both love and hate; to heal and to hurt; to be funny or to be sad. Some of us are just better at it than others. Even the least spiteful person in the world has spite. They just temper it instead of releasing it.

Our past is the gateway to the decisions that we all make about the constraints we will put on our own personality. If we find that we have been hurt time and again then we will choose to be less open and receptive in the future. If we focus drastically on the negative for long enough our expectations become cynical. Our past then is what leads to the immaculate separation of the human soul.

The chaos around us is controlled by the fact that each person, with his or her own selfish needs and desires, is working together in harmony with everyone else. The ups must one day equal the downs. The peaks eventually need to be as drastic as the troughs in order to bring about equilibrium.

So what is it that brings people together? How does a collective work alone, but in unison? What strings together the personality and actions of Elinore to anyone else? How is someone like Elinore connected to someone like Andrea?

Andrea is a thirty-one year old woman who has lived on her own in the same apartment for over twelve years. It is not as though she has not had the tendency to move. It is just that the apartment was her *first* apartment and she is the type of girl who likes to hold onto the important things in her life.

She works in a small office for a bastard of a boss but she is not exactly sure what they do. Her demeaning supervisor keeps insisting that it would be too complicated for her to understand even if he took the time to explain it. That category of statement understandably frustrates her a great deal. Presumably, all that Andrea is required to know is the accurate procedure needed to correctly complete the million and one invoices that cross her desk in an average day.

In complete contrast to Elinore, Andrea is a very striking woman. Her slender body is accentuated to look more sexy by the style of fashion that she wears. Her choice to cling involuntarily to a more natural look comes from her very strict mother. Andrea's beauty comes across as genuine and is often overlooked because of her refusal to accent her looks with cosmetics.

It is now twenty-five minutes after seven and Andrea is huddled in utter silence sitting in her favourite chair underneath the hanging reading lamp in the living room. She is wearing a light black, loose fitting pair of cotton pyjama pants with a faded grey shirt. Her arms are loosely folded across her chest.

Though the city is in efforts of waking up, Andrea finds pure content in her relaxed atmosphere and feels no strain what so ever of fatigue.

It should be mentioned that Andrea suffers from insomnia though such a declaration is a tad misleading. Andrea does not suffer because she has always enjoyed the fact that she can stay up late at night and observe the world with its deep tranquillity.

Her justification trickles into the notion that she has an extra eight or nine hours each day to accomplish all of her daunting errands. In spite of this additional time Andrea usually resorts to either following a mental concept to the very end in her head or thoroughly exploring ridiculous topics. This morning she spent roughly five hours contemplating the severe psychological problems of the person who insisted on naming the act of urinating, "number one".

By humorously naming the act she finds that it is trivialised and made to look less important than it truly is. Andrea understands that the intensions were to speak euphemistically so that the topic came across as less vulgar. Still, there is little doubt in her mind that this benefit is far outweighed by the controversy it may cause.

She wondered if the person who first coined the phrase did not realize that people have died from not doing a "number one".

An instinctive sixth sense from within alerts Andrea to the pressing issue of time. She drops her head ever so slightly moving the minimum amount necessary to check her watch which is tightly strapped around her left wrist. With an exaggerated sigh Andrea lifts herself to her feet. While stretching her lean body she staggers to the bathroom. She disrobes quickly and checks her hair in the mirror before opening the shower door.

In order to keep the water from splashing onto the floor she twists the shower head towards the inner wall and turns the taps to their appropriate settings. Her memory of the settings is a benefit of her loyalty to the apartment.

Allotting time for the water to heat up Andrea sticks her hand in the now warm water and enters the shower. There is a routine for showering to which she feels obligated to adhere. She is true to herself.

Once the shower is complete Andrea shuts off the water and waits for a second while watching the droplets fall by her feet. Before exiting the stall she wipes away much of the excess water with her hand and twists her hair attempting to squeeze it dry. After pushing open the door she walks out into the warm, steam filled bathroom.

Taking the towel from the hook beside the sink she dries herself off completely. Andrea grabs the housecoat that is hanging on the door and puts it on while gathering her clothes. It is a soft cotton robe, and it hugs her warm figure. Another habitual check in the mirror before leaving for her bedroom.

The glance is in vain because the mirror is completely steamed over from top to bottom. If her intentions were to actually see herself she would wipe away a section of the mirror through which to peek but she is comfortable with the incomplete action. Andrea consciously leaves the door ajar allowing an opportunity for the mist to dissipate.

After picking out an adequate outfit for the day she grabs a small purse and stuffs in it an extra pair of underwear and a second brazier. Curiously, she spends about as much time picking out both sets of clothing. Her night outfit is callously thrown into the hamper beside her dresser.

Andrea walks back into the living room, drops the purse onto the table then walks back into the bathroom to again hang her housecoat and to groom herself. By this time just enough steam has left for her to see her conspicuous reflection in the mirror. The dull haze of the mirror's image flatters her but she does not notice.

She grabs her brush and softly runs it through her partially damp hair. While tilting her head to one side Andrea starts to dry the hair with her five-watt hairdryer that her mother bought for her when Andrea was eleven.

About five or ten minutes later she comes out of the bathroom, gathers her necessities from the table and walks out the door locking it behind her. Just as Andrea is leaving the man in apartment four nineteen walks onto the elevator. A smile overpowers her face as a result of her good fortune.

Calling out to him to save the elevator she quickens her pace and plunges inside. Once in motion she thanks him and asks if he has had a good morning so far.

"Well to be honest, I'm running a little late and I believe that I'm going to miss my bus."

The statement burrows into Andrea a little. If they were good friends or old college room mates she could see how the man might give such a response. The fact is that he has lived in the building up the hall from her for over seven years and has not once ever tried to initiate a conversation. In the early stages of their living arrangement it appeared as though he may have even taken steps to avoid her. Unfortunately she lacked any proof of her suspicions.

What is even worse is that for the past two years Andrea has noticed that they ride together on the same bus to and from work. She merely asked her question to be both polite and friendly. It seemed as though it was the right thing to do. The least that could be expected of him is to return the favour and respond with what most people in civilized countries around the world and everyone inside the walls of the European block expect him to say.

"It has been a fine morning thank you and how are you?"

Andrea smirks at his behaviour. She hesitates for a moment to add a sense of drama then responds to the man's earlier snip.

"Oh I'm sure that the bus driver knows better than to leave with out you, don't you think?"

It is a clever retort. It not only forces the issue that *he* started but aggressively mentions that she is fully aware that he too takes the bus. Without even catching her sarcasm he replies.

"You never know these days. All those guys care about is that cheque that they get every Friday."

The door opens and without a seconds notice the man races out with the form one would only think possible of an elderly speed-walker. Andrea on the other hand takes her time.

The bus stop is about one hundred to one hundred and fifty feet north of their building. On this particular morning the sun is shining brightly and it is quite warm for the early time of day. Andrea arrives at the bus stop and turns to notice that the public motor vehicle is stuck behind the traffic light.

To force the issue even further with the man from room four nineteen she speaks to him with a piercing sarcastic tone.

"Who does this bus driver think he is? You've got a job to get to and *he* gets stuck behind the lights."

The man pretends to not hear and checks his watch almost searching for something to do. As the light changes and the traffic starts to move the bus arrives and the two file on one after the other. They pay their money and take their seats at either end of the bus with the man in front and her in the back.

As is often the case, Andrea is having some trouble letting the minor altercation rest. While taking her seat she imagines the man getting up and confronting her about the attack she made on him. It takes her a couple of attempts to get it right.

The first time he gets up is aggressive and quick. She agrees to herself that he is not as confrontational and would probably not approach in such a manor. Next, Andrea pictures him standing and looking back at her. There is a moment where it looks as though he is questioning whether or not he should go back.

This too seems wrong. Certainly the man would be upset. If he were to confront her at all he would not bring attention to himself while deciding. It would logically be a decisive action to either confront Andrea or to remain seated.

The way that it would most likely transpire is for the man to lean forward and look back at her. His decision to approach would be definite but the preliminary glance might be part of his strategy. He looks like a strategic man. Andrea would see the man and naturally glance back. Then he would calmly rise while mentally collecting his thoughts. His pace would quicken as he approaches her in the back of the bus, for appearance more than anything else.

"I don't know what your problem is this morning but I don't appreciate it. I was polite. I held the door for you. I made pleasant conversation. Did you not sleep much last night?"

"Oh go sit down."

If after seven years he did not know that she was an insomniac, Andrea is not going to be the one to tell him.

"If you don't…"

The man is stopped before he can continue his thought. Andrea squints her eyes both in her fantasy and in reality.

"How dare you. You know what your problem is?"

"No. And I don't want to hear it."

"I am going to tell you anyway."

"Well that figures. You always shoot your mouth off don't you?"

"How would you know? You don't know anything about me. That is your problem."

"My problem is that I don't know you? That is a little self centred don't you think?"

"It isn't me. What I mean is that you don't try to get to know me. You never try. We have lived in the same building for…"

"Well have you tried to get to know me?"

Again, in both states her head moves back to a more defensive position. Before she responds her face softens.

"You don't get it do you? It is not the effort. It is the intention."

Andrea loves being condescending in her own mind.

"What do you mean?"

"I mean that we never clicked. That is fine. I don't have to mix with everyone in our small corner of the country. But you don't even work with intention."

In her mind the man is showing the signs of regret. She presses on.

"The way you come across is as if I have offended you. Like something I did or said, maybe even years ago, has scarred you. You are not pleasant. You act impolite…"

The squabble erupts into a long, extracting debate. The man commences defending himself and Andrea sites numerous examples to prove him incorrect. Once she realizes that she has the upper hand she belittles him desperately but with much assumed subtlety. She then pictures what he would say against the attack and again what her reply might be.

A fit of anger and revenge glimmers in Andrea's eyes as she argues silently in her mind. Her head will sway from one side to the other to presumably keep straight the different speakers. Andrea is consumed by her imagination.

The wary victim to her overbearing subconscious is the ninety-minute drive in the conscious. The man from room four nineteen lay verbally slain in her head. In hindsight, it is good that he approached her the way that he did. The attack may have been worse with one of the other types of approach.

Again, her sixth sense snaps her back into reality with minimal reaction time remaining for her scheduled departure from the public mode of transportation. Andrea notices that her nemesis has already left. His path out the front was simple. Andrea, on the other hand, carefully slides her way through the amassed sea of bodies to the back door of the bus just before the door closes.

Even though the man from her building is not looking, Andrea passes him on the way into the office and delivers to him a very dirty look. She walks with an edge of satisfaction.

The room inside her place of work looks silent. The decibel level is certainly in a comfortable range but the appearance of the room is as though it is in a noiseless vortex. Completely unaware of the external she hops to her desk and places her bags behind the chair. In order to catch up on the left over invoices from the day before Andrea begins working immediately.

There are always invoices left from the day before. The nature of the business, whatever that may be, is that invoices are sent throughout each business day. Invoices received after the bank reconciliation time will not be processed until the following day. Though there are no more invoices than usual Andrea feels that today is different. She wonders if it has only been one night since being at work or if she has been away for some time.

Passing off the feeling as an unfortunate result of the problems that she had with her inconsiderate neighbour Andrea immerses herself in her work.

About two and half hours later she is tied up with a particular customer account as the telephone rings. While still attempting to process the bill Andrea answers the question of the frenzied lunatic on the opposite end of the telephone. She does not know who the person is or what he wants but she is tired of listening to his patronising tone. Andrea places the person in a frozen state by putting him on hold.

"Hold on and I'll transfer you to someone who can help you."

Of course there is no one else who can help because the only other person working in the office is Mr. Fitzpatrick, her boss, who is not currently present. He must have somehow forgotten that he owns the business and is probably somewhere in the downtown district handing in applications to be a stock boy.

Andrea takes a deep breath and stretches. It is her demonstration of a lighter mark of tension. She looks at the clock to examine the time and again begins to complete the paperwork.

The reason that she could not fill out the form completely was because she needs a document number from the filing cabinet so she moves to retrieve it.

Mr. Fitzpatrick enters and greets her. His voice is powerful and his mood is glorious.

"Good morning."

Her response is immediate.

"There's somebody on line one for you. Something about the Employer of the Year Award?"

Sarcasm unnoticed.

"I'll take it in my office."

Mr. Fitzpatrick walks into his bureau and closes the door. With a smile of satisfaction Andrea locates the missing document number and returns to her desk to complete the invoice from before. About ten or fifteen minutes later Mr. Fitzpatrick storms out of his office and screams at her.

"What the hell do you think you're doing?"

The act startles her so much that her hand slips and runs a crooked line through some of the documents on her desk. Andrea wants to complain about his actions, but does not. Her initial reaction is to reply with a question of her own. She does so without thinking further.

"What are you talking about?"

Attempting to avoid an argument Andrea chooses to keep her eyes lowered. She focuses on the paperwork but does not really watch it. It is as though she is looking through the paper.

"Who do you think was on the phone?"

"I don't know, it was just some guy that was screaming for the bastard in charge."

Andrea likes to think of herself as cool under pressure. This is truly not the case.

"That was the husband of the woman I was seeing about three months ago."

Mr. Fitzpatrick is referring to the affair that he was having. It was an affair with which Andrea was having much trouble. Technically it had nothing to do with Andrea. She was neither asked to lie nor was she asked to cover for either Mr. Fitzpatrick or the adulterous woman. Andrea just likes to keep a certain level of naiveté. Immoral behaviour makes that certain level hard to maintain.

"Who? I don't remember that."

"Remember? Yes, you remember. Rachel, the girl who had that thing on her chin."

"I thought that you broke it off with her."

Subtle as it may seem she has already started to change the subject. Andrea is very good at changing subjects while fighting. She does it to avoid the confrontations.

"Well I did, but I guess he's the jealous type. The guy threatened to come down and beat the crap out of me thanks to you."

Usually Andrea would forget this condemnation but with the mishap between her and the man from room four nineteen she is simply unable to.

"Listen. You don't pay me enough to apologize to every Tom, Dick or Harry that you piss off. Just because you can't score with anyone except those women who are put off men after living with their sick husbands for about fifty years, doesn't mean…"

Her boss successfully stifles her with his hand.

"Wait a minute here. Are you really complaining about having a job, because if you are you know, I can fix you up?"

Mr. Fitzpatrick always makes mindless threats to Andrea. She thinks that it is a power struggle that he likes to have. In actuality it is on account of his beliefs of socialism within a capitalistic market.

"Oh goodness no. I'm thrilled to earn a dime over minimum wage and be forced to listen to your crap day in and day out."

They have a good enough rapport with one another where they can be honest in a sarcastic dialect.

"You can't say that I've really treated you badly. I know that the job entails some unusual aspects…"

"Unusual aspects? That is a laugh."

He continues unaffected.

"...but it's because the business is new and I'm just getting started. You should be happy that you have a job at all."

Deep down Andrea knows that the dynamics of the town leave few possible employers. However, her complaint is not about the work. Why is it that occupations have to be accompanied by corporate cultural politics? Still, Andrea loves driving home a point with subtle cynicism. What she loves even more is that the entire discussion has been changed.

"A job that pays me less than half of what I'm worth, with a little more than twice the responsibility. You really know how to make a crappy situation look a whole lot worse, don't you?"

"Sometimes I wonder what you want in a job, Andrea. I let you use the phone for personal calls. I give you an extended lunch hour, job security and a cheque at the end of every week."

Andrea sees the silhouette of an opportunity from his poor choice of words.

"You know that I'm living from cheque to cheque. Can't you just give me a little raise?"

There is a slight pause in the conversation where it is possible to see that he feels a nerve of sympathy for Andrea. The wheel in Mr. Fitzpatrick's head is turning and working the figures of a few extra dollars each week for his loyal associate. With the stern emotion of a mortician he whispers his response.

"I just don't think that I can afford it."

Andrea drops her head with true emotion.

"Well I guess that makes two of us."

He cannot see her expression. Usually she is easy to read once you split through her mixed messages but her defences are raised.

"What does that mean? Are you quitting on me? You are so irresponsible."

She ends the argument quickly, fearing that she may not have the strength to justly campaign.

"Oh don't kid yourself; you'd never last without me."

She attempts the light-hearted joke to cheer herself up.

"You must be kidding; I could replace you in a minute."

There is a trace of sincerity in his speech. It is because of his belief system that he truly feels justified with his statement though on a personal level he would never like to prove the theory that he could replace Andrea in a short period of time.

Andrea's expression turns self-protective. Her words give her backbone.

"So why don't you? Huh? Why don't you? You are the cheapest, most despicable defornestor that I have ever seen in my…"

Mr. Fitzpatrick again raises his hand invoking silence.

"Hold on a second. I'm a what?"

Andrea is now both defensive and puzzled.

"What?"

"You said that I was a cheap…"

Mr. Fitzpatrick pauses to signify that there is something expected to follow.

"I said that you are a cheap defornestor."

"What the hell is a defornestor?"

Without losing her tone of anger she explains.

"You know. A defornestor. It means that you are a crook or a charlatan."

"There's no such word as 'defornestor'."

Andrea stays silent. Once he acknowledges that she is speechless he continues.

"God. I hate arguing with you. You are always making up these idiotic words that don't exist."

"I do not."

"You do too. It's like arguing with a creature from another planet. You never know what the hell it means when it says something to you."

In a lower voice she responds.

"I don't do that."

He continues to speak but not necessarily in the direction of Andrea.

"You can't argue with someone who makes up words. It's not fair. How could you? Even if you yelled back they wouldn't know what *you* were saying. And even though Andrea knows what I am saying she often pretends to misunderstand. Then when I explain myself again, ensuring that this time around she understands, she will throw in another new word, and the whole cycle begins again."

The argument has become rhetoric. He slowly leaves Andrea by herself and walks into his office again shutting the door, debating the issue with himself.

Mr. Fitzpatrick has a valid point. Andrea *is* the type of girl who will often create a word in a subconscious effort to stop an argument. People have the right to avoid arguments that disturb them through any means but this particular quirk has actually resulted in Andrea losing friends. The loss of friends was not only when Andrea was young and at the age when peculiar habits could banish one from others.

One of the friends that Andrea lost was a good friend of more than nine years. It happened no more than four months ago. Andrea does not know about the exact reason for the split yet. For her especially the loss of something so important adds quite a strain. A lot of pain is suffered by Andrea because of this loss but her fear of confrontation has held the issue unresolved to this day.

She recognizes that the argument with Mr. Fitzpatrick is over so she plummets back into the misery of her work. The contest is cast aside as another failed attempt to increase her salary.

At precisely five to twelve the watch on Andrea's left wrist pierces the silence that has accumulated over the last little while. The same silence from before. The silence to which one becomes accustomed with diverse noises in the background. The silence that only others cannot hear.

Andrea has set her alarm for a reason and as soon as she hears the chime a smile drapes over her face. Lunging for the telephone like a drowning man to a life preserver she instinctively dials seven digits. After a few rings a woman politely answers. Before the woman can utter any words at all Andrea vaults in and asks for Brian. Mr. Brian Donaccos.

The receptionist places the call on hold allowing time for Andrea to wonder whether or not she may have sounded a little immature. The first few words that she spoke were in a slightly higher pitch due to her excited state. While pondering the impression that she has left on the woman the deep voice of a man breaks her train of thought.

"Hello there Andrea, right on time I see."

The man knows that it is Andrea because she asked for him by use of his middle name. When his secretary informs him that someone has asked for Brian, instead of asking for his more common name Thomas, he knows that it must be Andrea.

There was a time not long ago when Andrea spent the night thinking about the secretary. Thanks to Mr. Fitzpatrick and the relationship that Andrea has with him, she relates to the secretary with a strongly felt bond. During a spell of insomnia Andrea wondered how the secretary was dealing with her own situation at work. She thought about conversations that the secretary may have had with Brian and the types of things that may have been said.

The romantic situation with Brian and Andrea is complex. It is imperative that Brian is fully aware at all times about from whom he is receiving a telephone call. His behaviour is different when speaking to his wife because his feelings about his wife are different than his feelings for Andrea. Even though it is possible that he would say the same things to both women over the telephone before realizing his mistake his wife would certainly notice a difference in his tone. It is a small issue that could lead to the unravelling of the complex situation.

"Are you kidding? I have been waiting for this call all day. I can't wait to see you. Are we still on for lunch?"

"Of course we are. I was hoping that you would let me take you to that new restaurant down on the corner."

"If we are still going to do what we talked about last Saturday then I would prefer it if we just grabbed pizza or a hamburger."

"Well I just thought that you would like a nice sit down meal first. But if you would prefer something simple, then why don't we just meet at that little pizza place next to the drug store. Then we wouldn't have far to go afterwards."

"That sounds good. I'm leaving now, okay?"

"I'll meet you there shortly. Alright? Bye-bye."

Andrea can faintly hear the click on the other end as Brian hangs up but she holds the receiver for a few extra seconds while passionately envisioning him rifling about in his office. Then with a sudden outburst of energy Andrea too returns the telephone receiver. Removing her bags from behind the chair she races out the door.

Her enthusiasm gets the better of her and she labours to stop herself from running. More than once while en route she checks her feet with astonishment.

The pizza shop is about two blocks from her office but she completes the journey in what seems like about four or five seconds even though it is most definitely not. The sun is still shining and the warmth of midday starts to settle in.

It would not have mattered to Andrea if she were standing inches from the eye of a horrible tornado. More precisely stated it would not matter to Andrea if she were standing inches from the most turbulent section of the tornado. The eye of the tornado is more often calm in relation to the swirling regions encircling it. It is also unlikely that such a situation would have no effect on Andrea but the meaning is that she is oblivious to most things around her because she has not seen Brian for over a week and she is concentrating only on their date. She wants to get as much as possible out of this rendezvous even if it means staring at Brian as he walks towards her amongst unfamiliar bodies.

Andrea is easy to read and her face begins to appear more disappointed with each passing moment; just like her classmate from the fifth grade, Jonathan Zibbel.

Jonathan Zibbel was a lonely student who sat by himself on hotdog day back in the fifth grade. It seemed as though everyone in the world knew that poor little Johnny would be the last person to receive his hotdog because of the predetermined decision to call upon students alphabetically by last name. However, after each name was called in succession Jonathan Zibbel fully expected an act of divine intervention from the hands of God delivering *his* hotdog next.

That is the way that Andrea looks though she does not know it. With every body that turns the corner her eyebrow raises in anticipation only to be let down again.

As it turns out Brian decided not to walk at all. He parked his car a short distance up the street and notices Andrea waiting for him. He approaches her from behind and cunningly sneaks up on her. His strong arms grab her tightly around her waist.

Knowing full well that it is Brian, Andrea raises her arms behind her head, folds them across his neck and sinks deeply into his awaiting figure. His reaction firmly asserts that he is not currently in a playful mood. Brian sharply dismisses her gaiety with a patronising kiss before lifting her back onto her feet.

Andrea turns to accuse Brian with her eyes but his thoughts have changed to something new leaving her attempt unnoticed.

"So, are you ready to eat Andrea?"

"Yes."

She speaks in an exaggerated sound of defeat as though she were speaking while sighing. It is another playful attempt at placing guilt on Brian for his cold actions, and it too is unsuccessful. The two of them walk into the pizza parlour almost like strangers. He holds the door for her, waits a second while scanning the contents of the street then casually walks in himself.

The short Italian man behind the counter approaches the two as they again become reacquainted. His appearance lacks professionalism but displays that he is ready to assist them with their order.

"O.K. Waddaya want?"

As the man looks up from his order pad he notices exactly with whom he is speaking.

"Ah. Mr. Donaccos. So nice to see you again. How is your wife?"

The man looks to Andrea and stops abruptly, realizing that Andrea is not Mrs. Donaccos. It is an error that could cause the man to reflect about the situation which could potentially lead him to disentangle the complex relationship. Brian does not hesitate to correct his blunder to alleviate any sense of embarrassment. Without the feeling that a mistake has been committed the man may not devote any more effort to the subject.

"My wife is lovely, thank you Salvatore. I will be sure to mention to her that I saw you today. For now though, I am afraid that I am in a bit of a hurry. You see I have to ensure that we get to the airport on time to have our distribution manager here, back in Los Angeles for tomorrow morning. You will forgive me won't you?"

Brian motions to suggest that Andrea is the distribution manager in question. The problem is that Andrea too is acquainted with Salvatore. Small town crowds give opportunity for many friends.

"Ah, Andrea. Congratulations. I did not know. I thought that you were still working for that Fitzpatrick fellow."

Andrea has no choice but to continue the charade.

"What can I tell you, Sal? They offered me more money."

There is an awkward pause for everyone. The first of the two patrons who speaks is Andrea.

"I don't know. What do you want Brian?"

After giving the menu his undivided attention he responds.

"Well. How about an eight slice with Pepperoni and...No, wait. Sausage, pineapple and extra cheese."

"You have got to be kidding me."

"What?"

"Since when have you ever liked pineapple on your pizza?"

The man behind the counter grimaces with wonder at the idea of how Andrea would know Brian's choice of toppings presumably having only worked with him a short time.

"Well I'm just in a pineapple kind of mood, that's all."

Andrea speculates if it is entirely possible to have *that* sort of mood. What might it mean to have a pineapple kind of mood? Would it be different from, say, a mood *for* pineapple? It is fuel for another lonely night.

Andrea ignores the man behind the counter because she believes Salvatore to be smart enough that he will catch on to their hoax anyway. She is in a playful mood.

"You know damn well that pineapple has no place being on a pizza. We're not living in Hawaii are we?"

Brian curls his mouth as though disappointed in his loss. Andrea continues to tease him trying to coax a reaction.

"Have you ever even had pineapple before? It is primarily a cold dish. You know, fruit? Should we add some apples to the list? Because apples might go nicely with the pizza sauce. And I don't know if they are in season but we can ask Sal if he can warm up some bananas for us to enjoy on the side. Hot fruit. That is what you are into?"

Brian snidely shakes his head. He is still much less playful.

"Fine then, why don't we just take an eight slice with sausage and extra cheese?"

Salvatore pretends to be busy with something else as Brian looks harshly into Andrea's eyes as if to ask for her approval. All that Brian does receive is the bitter cold bite of silence. True silence.

Brian is not the type of guy whose heart bleeds over the idea of Andrea eating a meal that she does not thoroughly enjoy. He takes the silence as a gesture of contention and places the order.

Andrea slowly turns and with her eyes to the floor walks to the corner of the shop with a couple of chairs. She puts her bags underneath one and sits down with a thump curled over with distinctly poor posture.

Andrea intently watches as Brian pays for the pizza. Her mind passes over the events that have just occurred. Her true intentions were never to disturb Brian. She was simply trying to start a playful episode by coaxing a reaction.

Andrea's guilt begins to explode because she understands Brian and knows that he is an emotional man. Brian could be potentially hurt from the detail of Andrea not being fond of the same toppings.

In reality, Thomas Brian Donaccos is the type of guy who could get a telephone call from the police informing him that his mother had just been killed after colliding with a drunk driver; and click over to answer the beep.

It is Brian's appearance that fools the gentle hearts like Andrea's. He is a massive, dark and handsome man who has relocated from Greece no more than six years ago. His charm is his ticket and it was quickly cashed in on Mrs. Gina Higgins. Gina is a naive business woman by default who inherited millions of dollars and who nearly jumped into Brian's arms allowing Brian to sweep her off of her wrinkly, old feet.

Brian's eyes are chestnut brown and the underbrush of a five o'clock shadow protrudes with masculinity about his chiselled chin. His well kept body is seductively masked in the expensive suits that he wears every day to his token job at Gina's office.

His Greek accent drives the women mad but was not easy for him to develop. Brian did not speak his first words until the second day of kindergarten. Even after that day he was quite a silent child.

His father thought that Thomas suffered from a sort of mental impairment. His mother, on the other hand, was convinced that Thomas's involuntary speech was rooted in *her* ethnic heritage. His mother's family was English and it was contemplated that Thomas was having trouble adapting to the Greek dialect because Thomas had an English mind like his mother. Though born in Greece, Thomas's mother felt that Thomas could not translate the language because of an English mind.

The most amazing attribute about Thomas is his demeanour. It instinctively does not allow him to come across as pompous or conceited even though it is the pit of his peach. He is so self-contained that he often mistakes the blatant boasting of another egomaniac as a desperate cry for his help and expertise.

To be quite honest he had not even noticed that Andrea had objected to his initial order. He was, at the time, checking his reflection in the large metal ovens behind the counter. As usual

Andrea is mistaking a sweet sensitive guy for a man who is passionate in bed.

Still at the counter paying for the meal, Brian collects his change then turns to Andrea. She gives him the kind of smile that would comfort a grieving child. He approaches her steadily and sits on her left but the manor with which he squats looks ungainly. There is an obvious attempt by Brian to balance his body over the sliver of his rear that connects with the chair in efforts of preserving his luxurious clothing.

They sit for a second in silence. It is a silence that would not be considered lumbering but one that awards them the time to reacquaint themselves with one another. Andrea uses the time to study his distinctive features. She follows his jaw line, stares at his stubble and pictures his pectoral muscles under his double-breasted jacket.

Thomas ponders a simpler dilemma: Whether he will get four slices or five?

Wiping away her subtle smirk Andrea whispers in a voice only Thomas can hear.

"You know we could have gotten the pineapple if you really wanted it. It's not like I would have left you for something *that* small."

He quickly replies, and with a voice slightly louder than hers.
"Sure."

Thomas pauses to signify his changing topics then continues.
"So are you, like, hungry or what?"

Andrea stops herself before cringing. The wound that she created becomes unmistakable. Brian is just *so* sensitive and a vow to right the wrong is solemnly sworn. She recognizes that he is trying to change the topic so Andrea prepares herself to be the bigger person by avoiding the conflict. In actuality there is no conflict to be avoided. It is also questionable if the avoidance would truly denote her as the more mature of the two people involved. Completely ignoring his question from before she asks how long he has for lunch before needing to return to the office. Since the attention remains with him, Brian too ignores his initial question.

"I'm done for the day."

Andrea surmises from this information that Brian has planned a special event. Her incorrect assumption also erroneously explains why he originally wanted to start with a romantic dinner rather than indulge in a quick lunch. She is of the opinion that Brian desires more out of the day.

Andrea's mind takes it another step. Recalling that Brian had voluntarily submitted to the less formal meal Andrea understands more thoroughly his hurt feelings with her playful tease. He has expended great effort in preparing the romantic day for the two of them that she has disassembled one element at a time.

First she quashed the idea of the romantic formal lunch. Then, by facing in the wrong direction she spoiled the sense of romance that one experiences when approaching a loved one. There is a stereotypical, slow-motion scene in many movies that screens two hopelessly infatuated lovers rushing towards one another with open arms. This is what Andrea thinks that Brian wanted as they met to eat. The pain that he would have felt when she teased him about his choice of toppings for the informal meal must have been disheartening.

"Oh."

She smiles at the fact that Brian left work for the day so that they could be together, but lowers her head with disappointment when she remembers that she is *not* done for the day.

"Oh, but I have to be back to work before one."

His response is a very simple.

"Oh."

Andrea feels terrible. He is going through a lot of effort to be with her and she is leaving the day incomplete. There is a large part of her that begins to feel regret for having teased him before.

His real disappointment is that he actually thought that Andrea needed to be back earlier than one o'clock. Brian's plans include the completion of a few minor tasks neglected throughout the week which now might not be finish until later than anticipated. His silence is due to the required time needed to update his mental daily planner.

A while passes before Salvatore beckons Andrea and Brian to the counter to retrieve the pizza that has finished cooking. Andrea grips her baggage and waits by the door while Brian accepts the pizza with a polite nod. Neither Brian nor Andrea is concerned about Salvatore or the revealing conversation from before. They leave the store promptly walking beside one anther towards Thomas's car.

As he often does, Brian tenders to Andrea the keys for his lavish automobile; and as always, Andrea agreeably accepts them. It causes her to experience the same nervous trembling in her stomach from the matter of Brian's trust which she considers being a sentiment of his loyalty.

His true motivation is not loyalty but is selfishness. Thomas only wants the opportunity to eat at a quicker pace. The arrangement also works in his favour because he very much hates to drive. The stress is something to which he has never become accustomed.

They enter the car and prepare to drive away by routinely applying their seat belts. Actually, Andrea lays the belt around her body properly but Thomas only wraps the strap around his shoulder. This assembly would have no ability to secure him in the event of a major car accident.

The minor assistance from Thomas's seat belt is only for the benefit of a potential encounter with the law. From behind, it would appear that both Andrea and Thomas are properly fastened to their seats in accordance with current safety regulations. Andrea pretends to not notice as a usually embarrassing noise resonates from Brian's stomach. Answering the call he crams the first piece of pizza forcefully into his mouth.

Andrea carefully looks in all directions before gearing into drive, heading to a motel not far away. The car is parked in the opposite direction of the motel with respect to the pizza shop. In fact the car is parked farther up the street from the pizza place than is the motel situated down the street in the other direction. It would have taken less time to walk to the motel but Thomas did not want to risk sweating in the embracing, warm sun as they retrieve the automobile afterwards.

The traffic is light and Andrea pulls into the motel parking lot as Thomas is shoving his third piece of pizza into his mouth. She kindly turns to him.

"I'll let you off here to get the room, okay Brian? And I'll go park the car behind the motel so that nobody drives by and recognizes it."

Thomas lifts his mouth slightly to keep the food from falling out. His reply is concise.

"Yep."

He snatches another piece of pizza before exiting the car to apparently give him the strength required to complete the journey up the steps of the motel and through the door to the front desk.

If Andrea was absorbedly watching, her mind would no doubt be active. She might imagine scores of people clapping, motivating Brian to complete the journey. A police officer would be watching the crowd and stopping traffic for the big event. There might be a couple of elderly volunteers huddled just in front of the masses with juice and water for Brian because the journey would have left him dehydrated. A large clock overhead would give his final time result, accurate to a tenth of a second from Swiss craftsmanship. He might collapse at the top of the steps from exhaustion but would recover to finish the race. Unfortunately Andrea was not paying attention.

Thomas exits the automobile and bumps the door shut with his hip. Once clear of the car, Andrea steps on the gas to cruise around back just as she had cleverly planned. She pulls into what she considers to be the perfect spot. It is a fairly large space between an old, blue pick-up truck and a dark grey station wagon.

Andrea is not sure of the exact model of the station wagon because the general design of the car has not changed much over the years. There is a moment when she scours her memory questioning if only a single manufacturer ever produced the station wagon. She wonders if there are in fact different models for wagons or if they are more like wine from a French vineyard. Perhaps there is just a vintage for station wagons. Maybe the producer alters the models each year and somewhere in the world are connoisseurs who debate a car when they see it.

"That is a classic '78, don't you agree?"

"I would, if only it were a '78. Look at the headlights. The '78 did not have that sort of technology."

"You are right. It is obviously a blend. I would say from an accident. Late fall of '84. The harmful corrective work must have been because of the limited supply of older headlight systems."

"I think that the car exhibits charm"

"You are talking crazy."

Andrea stops her fantasy not believing that a snobby connoisseur of vintage automobiles would use the term "crazy". She gets out of the car after retrieving her small bag with the extra pairs of undergarments and shuts the door. A brisk wind blows just as she attempts to close it which leaves the door slightly ajar.

Fighting back the urge to swear out of frustration she puts the bag in her left hand and with her right hand reopens the door. As she slides the keys into the lock she is transported back in time to when she was twelve years old.

She vividly recalls a scene in an old black and white film that she and her father watched the night that her grandmother died. The film contained an extremely beautiful woman who was being followed by the Soviet police. Every time the lady from the film would exit her car she would check over both her shoulders to see who was around.

Still in a playful mood, Andrea mimics the actions of the movie star but finds her performance a little disappointing and unrealistic. The closest comparisons to Andrea and the woman in the film are that they are both beautiful women, and that they both have blond hair. At least Andrea thinks that the lady had blonde hair. It is impossible to tell because the movie was in black and white.

There is no mystery anywhere in a town of this size. The Soviet police are not lurking around every corner. Andrea's imagination is not complimented by appropriate surroundings.

A few moments later Thomas pops around the bend and the two walk peacefully up to the room. After fiddling with the door for more than a minute Thomas hears the click of the lock and kicks the door open completely. Standing idle for a short time he itemises the contents of the room. Once comfortable with his new surroundings Thomas proceeds inwards.

Andrea gives the playful plot one more chance. Pretending still to be nervous about getting caught she looks around suspiciously and races in after him. Her anxiety, though fictitiously found, causes her to slam the door shut thus losing all the subtlety that they had tried so hard to create.

She drops her bag by the door with no further concern and with the high pitched squeal of a pig tackles Thomas onto the bed. She grapples with Brian, moving him from his side onto his back. Using her leverage to hold him down allows her the time to force her body on top of his chest.

With her legs dangling over the sides of his torso she leans forward, takes hold of his wrists, and pins them to the stiff cushion. Andrea looks down at Brian with the air of someone who has just conquered a large mountain and smiles her seductive smile.

"I've been waiting to do this all week."

With no struggle at all he relocates his hands to a position that enables him to use his elbows. He pivots above his back and lifts his upper body. Then, by dropping his left shoulder he turns his body just enough to make Andrea slide right off of him and onto the mattress.

Admitting defeat she lays back with open arms and the two embrace with a kiss. It is an emotional kiss that sends a current of electricity directly to Andrea's brain. As the passion ignites she again becomes aware of the silence that fills the room.

The relationship that she is in is one which most would consider immoral. At the very least the relationship would be considered unethical. However, Andrea admires the relationship that she is in. It is not about being right or doing the right thing. It is about the right thing happening and in the right way. Andrea has never really had a relationship that most people would deem good. Her prior romantic couplings could not have endured the silence that she and Thomas are enduring now.

Thomas gently grasps her cheek and forces Andrea to switch the side on which she is kissing. Forced to break her train of thought, Andrea obliges him then continues with a flashback.

His name was Trevor. Back in the eleventh grade Andrea and Trevor were known as *the* popular couple. People in the halls of the school would often talk about them and there had been more than one conversation about the pair at lunchtime in the cafeteria.

Andrea remembers Trevor asking her out in grade nine but recalls delaying acceptance until midway through the tenth grade though the situation is wrong for her to presume. It was in fact a different boy who propositioned her in grade nine. He was not different in a philosophical sense; in that we are all different people and that we grow and change. It was actually a different boy altogether.

The name of the other boy was strange. It is not a typical name. Not one that stands out anyway. It was always being mispronounced, or forgotten entirely. The name started with the letter "U".

The two boys did look alike. The major difference was that Trevor was much more popular. The other boy did not have many friends at all. For some reason, he was under the impression that Andrea had an interest in him. It hurt him dearly when Andrea turned him down. The boy switched schools not long after Andrea broke his heart. Though the odds are not good, there is a chance that while

Andrea is having a flashback about the boy, somewhere in the world, something is causing him to have a flashback about her.

Andrea used to tease Trevor about the misunderstanding. She thought that it was endearing how he would deny having been initially turned down by her. In actuality, he was denying the fact that it ever happened. In his case he is right because it never did.

Trevor and Andrea met when a friend of Andrea started dating a friend of Trevor. Andrea insisted on having a double date. It was not about dating Trevor necessarily. She had heard good things about double dates and she wanted to experience one. Her friend necessitated and the rest is inaccurate history.

The thing about their relationship was that Trevor always insisted on playing the radio every time they began to kiss. No matter where they were. If they were at a party, in the car, in his house or outside when they began kissing, music had to be playing.

One time Trevor even made them wear earphones and listen to his walkman because his radio was broken. He passed it off as a romantic gesture by claiming that he had made the tape for Andrea with their favourite songs, but he had not. Andrea knew that he had not.

Andrea imagines Trevor peering through the window watching the two of them kissing fervently. Though years have passed since high school she imagines Trevor looking exactly the same as he did in grade eleven. She vividly pictures him mouthing words of protest. She would obviously not be able to hear him say the words.

"God, those two must really be in love. There not watching television, or anything."

Without admitting to herself that she is corny Andrea redirects her concentration back to Thomas. It would be apparent to anyone who has ever been involved with another person that *these* two people clicked. There is never any of that awkward fumbling that most people have in the bedroom.

Thomas and Andrea are like psychics. Psychics who use their powers best when trying to undress one another. They never rush the other person and yet they never make the other person wait either. If ever there was a perfect time to commence disrobing your partner these two would find it.

Smooth as silk too. No stuck zippers. No buttons that will not pop. Hooks seem almost to disengage themselves. When Andrea and Brian decide to undress one another they look as though a Hollywood magnate has scripted the choreography.

Andrea is convincing herself that she is in the middle of the most romantic afternoon of her entire life. She hits a point of romantic bliss and smiles strenuously. Thomas uses his upper body strength to set both of them into a more comfortable position on the bed. The surprise floats Andrea more. She lets herself act freely on wild impulses. After nudging his shoulder Thomas takes the hint and roles onto his back. She slithers her way on top and again switches the side on which they are kissing. It is a deep, wet, forceful kiss.

The face of Trevor at the window in her brain shows shock and discomfort. His jaw slumps as though expected to drop and his eyes bulge from their sockets, literally exaggerated by Andrea's mind. Her nerve endings are so sensitive that she can no longer continue to conjure up the imaginary, jealous ex-boyfriend.

Butterflies in her stomach whiz around so relentlessly that they bang into each other with ticklish delight. Every time that Andrea thinks that things cannot possibly get any better Thomas does something that stretches the boundaries of her romantic designs. Minutes melt together. Seconds stretch away. It is unfortunate that the fourth dimension has to govern two such magical bodies in the third.

Thomas, on the other hand, is not finding the encounter quite as romantic. For him romance is not something that you can plan. Romance stems from an overwhelming desire to please another person. It is frankly achieved by doing something completely out of the ordinary but under regular constraints. Romance is not grabbing a pizza and renting a motel room to have sexual relations. Sex and romance are barely linked. In fact they are nearly inverse, exclusive events. Nearly.

Though it may seem hard to believe, Thomas *is* the romantic type. That is not to say that he does not enjoy the occasional fling now and again. For him, romance is more of an action at which he considers himself to be good. It usually results in women swooning over him and if the end result is ever to have more attention directed towards himself then it is something that he likes.

It is terrible to admit that romance is subjective. One would hope that romantic tendencies are ever filling, and that the mere notion of a romantic act consumes one fully. It does not. Not for the naturals at least and Thomas is most certainly a natural.

If romance did not come naturally to Thomas then unquestionably, he would not be romantic. Andrea is using her overactive imagination to rub her happiness in the face of an old fling. It is her way of sharing the deep happiness that she is experiencing because the nature of their complex relationship does not permit Andrea to share it with many others. She is not a romantic natural yet even she is not consumed on the most romantic day of her entire life.

Brian's mind is busy trying to settle on the order with which to tackle the remaining activities of his day. He is figuring out whether to go to the bank first or to go to the grocery store and then to the bank once their rendezvous has ended. At least Andrea enjoys romance for its by-products.

Thomas's wife left instructions for him on his desk at work. He is supposed to pick up some food at the grocery store and tend to some business while at the bank. This is the real reason that Brian is done work for the day. His concern is that he has to go clear cross town to the bank before coming all the way back to the grocery store. Even worse is the idea of his return trip home being that their mansion is closer to the bank than it is to the grocery store.

Brian keeps trying to think of how much money he has with him. If he can afford the groceries without going to the bank beforehand then he will save himself the unnecessary trip. There is no real reason for Thomas to be in a hurry. It is not as though he has plans later in the day. The question becomes about the amount of effort that Brian is willing to extend to complete his required duties.

He cannot remember if he paid for the pizza with a twenty or with a fifty dollar bill. Brian is trying to remember how much money his wife, Gina Higgins-Donaccos, gave to him for the tasks. Unfortunately, he cannot make the recollection with enough certainty to ease his mind.

Once the passion ceases Thomas grabs excitedly for his wallet which is in the right side pocket of his pants. His pants, in turn, are in a heap on the nightstand beside the bed. He can faintly hear Andrea remarking about something that he has uttered just moments ago but he is unable to centre his thoughts because he is about to unravel the mystery of exactly how much money he does indeed have.

"I wish that I could just sit here in your arms forever, but I'm afraid that I have to get going soon."

Thomas opens his wallet. Andrea lays her hand on his shoulder summoning a reply.

"Damn it."

"What is wrong Brian?"

Thomas checks the thin collection of bills.

"I thought that…"

Andrea pulls him back to her. He wiggles his way onto the pillow with her arm comfortably beneath him. Andrea, now lying across his chest, stares upwards and into his eyes. She rubs his head with her free arm in support and puts her finger to his mouth motioning for him to stop. Thomas does stop because it has been taught to him from a very young age that it is inappropriate for one to discuss openly his or her financial concerns.

"I know. But I told you that I have to be back before one Brian."

They lay still for a short time. He is aware that she has misinterpreted his concern but he is too occupied by irritation to correct her. Still assessing his cash flow Thomas reaches for his pants again. He rifles through the left pocket and pulls out a muffled wad of bills and coins. Content with his findings he settles back into the comfortable arms of his mistress.

Andrea turns her wrist slightly and strains her eyes to check the time on her watch. Thomas notices her motion and understands her intensions.

"Well if you have to go, then maybe we should go."

"I don't have to go yet. I'm just saying that I have to be back before one."

Thomas checks his watch to see what is the time. He places the timepiece to his ear in disbelief thinking, maybe even wishing, that the day was farther along than his watch is showing. The problem is that with as expensive an article as it is he knows that the time is quite accurate. Resourcefully, he uses the extra minutes to create a mental checklist of his requirements from the grocery store. Andrea listens to the timing of their breathing patterns.

A short while passes before Andrea rises from the comfortable situation. She retrieves her bag from in front of the door and travels into the washroom to freshen up and to change into her spare undergarments. Returning from the washroom Andrea notices

Thomas gathering his clothes. They kiss quickly before he too enters the washroom to freshen up. She moves to the dresser where the almost empty box of pizza sits so that she can nibble briefly before getting back to the invoices at work.

While running the tap water with both hot and cold pressure Thomas rushes his hands underneath periodically checking the warming temperature. He does not like when cold water hits his body. He can hear Andrea moving about in the other room. She is tidying the area. His attention does not stay with her for too long and returns to his own reflection in the mirror.

After making himself quite presentable, in case he runs into anyone at either the store or the bank, Brian exits the bathroom leaving the light on for no apparent reason.

"Where are my…"

Thomas stops himself. Andrea is standing by the window holding his shoes. She is ready to leave, having finished the remaining slices of pizza. Thomas quickly puts on his shoes and reaches for his jacket. Andrea stretches to open the door but she is stopped.

"Not yet."

"What is wrong?"

Without speaking he slides into his jacket and checks himself in the mirror above the desk. He has a little fidgeting and rearranging before his is ready to be seen.

"Alright, are you ready to go?"

Andrea nods. She opens the door and waves him through. Thomas turns after exiting and witnesses her examining the room again to ensure that things are respectable and that she is not leaving behind anything of any importance. She follows him out and closes the door behind her.

"Wait!"

"What? What is the matter?"

Though the flaw took a moment to register she is troubled about something from the room.

"You left the bathroom light on."

Thomas looks at her with a serious expression.

"Are you kidding?"

He watches her blush without reaction.

"Stop teasing me. Fine. I guess it'll be alright."

Andrea puts her arm around Brian in a submissive stance. Thomas gives her a patronising pat on the back, to thank her for the hug, and then liberates himself. He races down to the automobile and starts the engine before she even successfully negotiates the steps from the second floor.

Pulling around to where the stairs meet the first floor he leans over and opens her side of the car. The door swings open about half way, but teeters. Andrea reaches for the door but checks at the same time over her shoulder for the Soviet police. Her odd behaviour causes her to miss the opportunity as her hand slides right over top of the door. It swings back and closes completely.

Andrea lifts the handle and situates herself inside the motor vehicle but before she can even close the door properly Thomas speeds away. There is no conversation between them. Thomas is perusing the landscape to sharply avoid any obstacles that could delay her delivery further. Andrea is consumed again with idle thoughts.

She wonders about her problem with the car door from a moment ago. Why is it that simple tasks like getting into a car while looking over your shoulder seems so uncomplicated in the movies? Understandably, the heroes or heroines of films need to look suave; but what about the everyday person? Does a person's inability to complete simple tasks make them look more primitive? What about the reality that films are supposed to be showing of life?

Throwing the lavish vehicle into neutral Thomas shoves open his door and scampers into the front lobby to return the key. Andrea turns to look inside and an overwhelming feeling of discomfort strikes her. It is not in reference again to the faltering with her entrance into the car. It is not about the argument with her neighbour from the morning, nor is it about the argument with Mr. Fitzpatrick.

She wonders about the front desk clerk. What sort of explanation is Brian giving for the short stay in the hotel? Is there an explanation at all? The deliberation sours her mood. She plays back the events of the afternoon in her head. The phone call. The quick lunch. The drive over. She revisits *that* light. The stupid light that she should have turned off. It would have been the right thing to do.

Still running, Thomas emerges from the building, hops into the car and drives away. He drives incredibly fast the entire distance to Andrea's office.

"You just blew that light Brian."

Brian checks the rear view mirror. Sure enough he has driven right through a red light. He peeks briefly at his own image before replying.

"Looked Yellow. Besides we don't want to be late, now do we?"

"But I would like to get there in one piece."

Her body language is screaming. Andrea is not scared but she is observably displeased with the afternoon. The tryst did not transpire as flawlessly as it should have, or as flawlessly as it did in her head.

"Would I ever let anything bad happen to you?"

She feels that he understands. Maybe he feels similarly to the way that she does. Maybe he too considered the afternoon to be a shade less than perfect. Andrea smiles at Brian in a way that makes him notice. She leans in to kiss him and he turns slightly to catch it on the cheek allowing him to keep an eye on the road ahead. It was not meant to be a sign of disinterest. They drive on until they are in front of her office building.

"I won't kiss you again, in case someone is watching. But thanks for the wonderful afternoon Brian."

They say their good-byes. Andrea sighs with relief before she departs.

"I will call your office the day after tomorrow."

"I can hardly wait."

Andrea does not question his sincerity. She should not, as he is being genuinely earnest.

"If you need to though, you can call me."

Thomas nods his head at the notion. He never contacts her first, though. He has to be discrete.

She accidentally slams the door with more force than anticipated and Thomas disappears progressively. The traffic has again thinned down. Most of the people are already back at work. Revisiting his plan from earlier, he sets off for the grocery store.

While en route Thomas turns on the radio. It is more than just a habitual act. He wants to find a good song. Music can relax Thomas and it can also get him into a better mood. He is not necessarily in a bad mood now but understands that one can always be in a better mood.

It is just turning one o'clock and every station known to mankind has interrupted their commercial free music with the same news report that they have been reporting for the last three hours. Regardless, he takes a trip around the band to see if any stations did not yet realize the time. His disappointment with the situation is not colossal. Thomas is not a real fanatic of music anyway. It has a certain effect on him but is more a derivative than anything else.

A lot of the technical aspects of music are lost on Thomas. He enjoys a few of the big band songs that have recently been released but the rock and roll that is most influential initiates agitation. He does not like live music and it is truly better that he does not listen to it. Thomas wants the polished version of the artist. The way that *they* want it to sound. He does not understand the intense work related to playing an instrument, and he does not care to. The energy of live music is unimportant to him and most times would go unnoticed anyway. Truthfully, Thomas wants the music industry to produce music for his entertainment. It is not an artistic outlet, or at least the artistic outlet is not for him.

He drives into the parking lot of the shopping mall and almost forgets why he has gone there in the first place. A runaway shopping cart nearly side swipes his car and jogs his memory. He peers to the front of the grocery store to see if there are any free parking spots. It is unusually busy for the time of day. His speed falls dramatically because most of his effort is spent looking for a choice parking spot near the entrance. There does not seem to be any open positions.

Thomas figures that it will be just as easy to park beside the grocery store, without the designated parking lines, as it would be to continue inspecting the lot in front. The delivery trucks usually drive through the side of the store, where he intents to park, in order to get to the back doors to deliver their product. Thomas does not plan to be inside the market for a very long time and believes that he has left plenty of room for the trucks to pass.

Before he enters through the sliding doors his attention is stolen. As though he had no other choice but to turn Thomas looks out to the lot. A gleam of light reflects off of the dark pavement from the two parking spaces now vacant at the very front, hitting him directly in his eyes. His mouth curls admitting that he really does not care.

Inside the store, he does not walk each aisle. Knowing the layout of the store allows him to navigate through the aisles for exactly those items that he requires. Very quickly he locates what he needs and joins the queue for the express lane.

Thomas does not get upset with the typical argument against the express lane. He admits openly however that it is really not fair to categorize the lane as an express lane, in that the term "express" has a definite connotation of speed. He just refuses to argue the point like so many others.

Everyone knows that it does not save much time. Most of the people pay with diminutive denominations and they always engage in some small talk with the cashier. It is also quite common for people with more than the maximum number of items to use the lane. Thomas even created an amusing game to play while in line at the market. When the mood strikes he likes to engage in an episode of Express Lane Mathematics.

Express Lane Mathematics occurs when patrons have the opportunity to count the number of items in someone's basket or buggy. It can be fun trying to figure out how the person justifies lining up in the express lane knowing full well that they have more than the maximum amount. Are bananas to be counted as individual items or are they sold as a single bundle? Would items that are marketed as being sold two for one be considered as a single purchase? Do related items require their own groupings? For example, cereal with milk or coffee with cream. Thomas is good with justification in general and he is especially strong with this sort of justification. He thoroughly enjoys himself while trying to figure it out. Today is different however and he does not take part in the sport.

It is not long before Thomas finds himself at the front of the line. The cashier smiles at him and opens her mouth signifying that she would either be open to polite pleasantries or if he would prefer, she too would talk in a brief conversation. He neither wants to nor does.

As he turns the corner after exiting the store he begins checking the grocery bags to be sure that he has bought everything that he needs. Now that he is getting on in age his mental checklists are not as exhaustive as they once were.

Standing in front of his car sticking his hand deeply into one of the bags his search is brusquely interrupted by a voice. It is not a scary voice but a loud, obnoxious voice that hollers at him.

"Alright buddy. Don't turn around. Just keep your mouth shut and give me your wallet."

Thoughts race through Thomas's head. He tries desperately to come up with the suitable way to handle a mugging. His heart starts thumping. A small lump forms in his throat.

"Hi, I'm Thomas."

Thomas rolls his head becoming a little embarrassed. Even he knows that his response sounds unintelligent. The voice replies in a condescending tone.

"Well, hello there. I'm the man who is going to rob you blind and leave you penniless in humiliation."

A hush soaks the background. Thomas feels the sarcasm hit him in his pride. The voice turns serious.

"Just keep your mouth shut and you won't get hurt."

Thomas leans up against his car while standing in front of the driver side door. The man behind him searches frantically through Thomas's pockets. As the mugger is reaching inside the expensive blazer to search the inner pockets Thomas rotates around just enough for him to catch a glimpse of the man.

It is not a man at all. It is a boy.

In relief Thomas rotates fully, now realizing that the man is in fact a seventeen or eighteen year old kid. A seventeen or eighteen year old kid with an alarming, elderly voice. In reality the boy's voice is not all that deep. It is funny how different things sound when one is afraid for his or her own life.

As soon as Thomas faces the boy the mugging halts. The kid is absolutely perplexed at the nerve of his victim. There is an exchange of confidence and Thomas speaks to him coldly.

"Listen punk, I don't care…"

Thomas too is interrupted. Interrupted not by the words of a more persevering youngster but by the fist of a feverish young man.

It must be noted that Thomas is not claiming to be a fighting sort of man. If the truth were known he is verily not inclined to take a punch of any magnitude. The swing knocks Thomas into a sort of drunken stupor and he falls back onto his performance automobile. He falls not from the sheer force of the punch but by his newly acquired state of disequilibrium.

Thomas is stunned for a second and awakens with a quick shake of his head. The pupils in his eyes strain to allow in the proper amount of light. He again becomes aware of the young man now searching his wallet for cash or anything else of real value. Thomas stands up straight again. He wobbles at first but gets to his feet progressively. Feeling the loss of the confidence he once had Thomas tries to reason with the boy.

"Listen, I don't know what you want, but I haven't got it."

It is another open season for sarcasm.

"But if you don't know what I want, then how do you know that you don't have it?"

The boy returns to rifling through Thomas's wallet. Perhaps it is not the best time for him to work with reason. Turning his head and raising his eyebrows Thomas is almost looking for an answer to the kid's rhetorical question. With a forceful tone the boy turns serious.

"Alright Mac, give me what you got."

Thomas's heart speeds up again as it is smacked with panic. His mind races. He tries to design different strategies for immediate action but nothing forms fast enough. There must be something that can get him out of this situation unharmed.

His adrenaline finally strikes and Thomas attempts to flee the scene like a dog avoiding the swift slap of the owner's hand. Jumping towards the larger body out of reflex, the boy cuts off the escape route and knocks Thomas back into the car.

Folding to the ground, Thomas winces in pain though he is not really hurt. He childishly collapses his arms inward, to his stomach. The young man grabs the limp body by his left shoulder and picks him up off of the ground. The boy would certainly not have had the strength to lift up the folded body under normal circumstances but Thomas is kind enough to assist. Thoughts of the boy's acrobatic moves course through both of their minds making special note of the teenager's remarkable agility. At least it seemed acrobatic to Thomas. The boy also thinks highly of himself because the move was so effective.

Bang. The youth slams his right fist aggressively into the cheek of his victim.

The wall of the store is completely blocking the sun's view of this action but the warmth remains and is felt by both Thomas and his assailant. Instinctively Thomas recoils from the beating that he is receiving but his mind is elsewhere. Thomas thinks to himself.

"Alright. I have seven dollars and eighty-seven cents left in my wallet. I guess that it was a good idea for me to do the groceries before heading to the bank."

Bang. The boy delivers another shot.

"Oh but I'll need my identification for the bank. Whatever I do, I'll have to keep that. He won't need my license anyway. And..."

Another bashing from the youngster interrupts his train of thought. Blood trickles down Thomas's nose and onto his lips. Thomas feels it but the pressing issue of his valuables takes top priority.

"Oh yes, I can't let him see my watch. That thing cost me over..."

The punches start arriving more frequently. The boy feels empowered. The large, fit man is falling victim to his scrawny build. For the time being Thomas forgets about the value of what he is losing and concentrates fully on whether or not he will make it out alive. It is an exaggeration of course but a logical step. This is the first time that anything similar to this has happened to Thomas and he does not actually know what to expect. His rationale is not quite clear. With all his might he musters up enough strength to force out an optimistic thought.

"Okay. He is punching me. Very hard mind you. I don't think that it will do any real…"

Another punch from the hands of the youth turns Thomas's head with an uncomfortable jerk.

"…harm. The way I see it is that it will hurt for about three or four days, but the bruising won't even be noticeable in a couple of weeks."

Just as he regains some confidence from this new notion the young man delivers an upper cut sending him flying back into the car. Adding insult to injury Thomas notices that the attack makes him bite his tongue. A throbbing bump starts forming on his jaw. Like an alcoholic turning to the power of God he returns to his argument.

"I'm twenty-nine years old now. There are fifty-two weeks in the average year. That makes, let's see, a little over fifteen hundred weeks. Relatively speaking, this injury won't even be noticeable for one percent of my lifetime."

Though the creator of Express Lane Mathematics, Thomas is not a mathematical genius. It is amazing how much clarity can result from surprise. The kid winds up and slams his fist hard against the temple region of Thomas's head. Falling to the ground mere moments from being unconscious a final thought completes itself.

"One percent. I can live with that."

The kid stands towering over Thomas's body in amazement. He did not expect the brawl to go so easily. Thomas is quite a solid figure.

Shrugging his shoulders in disbelief the boy speaks out loud to nobody in particular.

"I can't understand why he didn't even put up a fight."

The sun plays a villain to Thomas. Breaking through a cloud it wraps a ray around the corner from the front of the store. It passes the boy with an extra jolt of warmth and collides with the clasp of Thomas's expensive watch. The reflection of the watchband, now uncovered from the expensive suit, catches the eye of the mugger. The glimmer of the watch is exactly that of the glimmer of a statue on top of a trophy. The miscreant decides to leave the watch anyway. It would look too fancy on his skinny, diminutive wrist.

The mugger's name is Colin. Colin is about six foot, one inch and weighs about one hundred and fifty to one hundred and sixty pounds. His hair is not at all in fashion. It is a mullet which is the type of hair that a lot of hockey players wear. It is cut short along the sides and on top but is left long in back. Though he has the hair of a hockey player Colin lacks the dexterity to skate with any proficiency. Even if he did know how to skate his chain smoking would ensure that he would be out of breath before he even tied his laces.

His nose is slightly out of joint and has been ever since he fell down and broke it in the first grade. Colin had been running after his dog on the day in question. The lovable pet had escaped from the leash while they were walking and Colin panicked when the dog started racing after a squirrel in the park. It was amusing to witnesses but the dog was very serious about the pursuit.

The story is not one that Colin would ever let others know. He would probably explain that his dad had beaten him for swearing or for committing another minor offence, but a fable of an emancipated canine *is* the truth.

Colin's eyes are dark green and the rest of his body is emaciated. He is wearing tattered clothing that closely mimics the clothing of other children of the street- the runaway sort of kids with their weather-beaten attire. Kids who often wear a heavier cloth to help keep them warm on cold, hard nights. Garments that are stained in various spots and which are in dire need of a good cleaning.

Yet Colin is not a street kid. His past is not the type of past that one would consider being riddled with psychologically disturbing activity. His family is not poor. They are not exactly upper class but they are comfortable financially.

Colin did not have a bad childhood. He did not totally enjoy his childhood; but he did not have the type of childhood that is understood to be the instigator of poor, socially unaccepted behaviour. He did not enjoy his infancy because it was different from the type of infancy that he dreamed of having. The grass for him was always greener elsewhere, so he grew up metaphorically cutting down his own. Colin was raised in a middle class neighbourhood with many friends. Good friends. Not good friends of his but friends that, in any other social circles, one would consider fortunate to have.

His parents supported his efforts at learning the trombone. They supported but did not force. The decision was always Colin's to make. A proficiency of the trombone is certainly not a fact that he would have anyone know.

Standing there in front of the unconscious stranger, Colin begins to feel pity. After taking the money from the wallet he throws the stylish article down by figure's head. Without concern for prosecution of his actions Colin patiently leaves down the alley behind the store. He sneaks behind one of the dumpsters and slips through a loose board in the wooden fence.

His pace slows even more as the heat from the sun is catching up with him. Colin points his head to the ground as he curiously watches his feet pass one another. The narrow view of his feet reminds him of a close-up in a movie sequence. His feet blur as they pass one another in action.

Sliding down a couple more side streets he finally arrives at his building. It is a run-down, brown building of twenty stories. It looks as though it might fall at any second.

In his pocket are his keys. Colin reaches for them but takes his hand out of his pouch without the keys once he sees the fat woman from the sixth floor waddling her way down the corridor. He rocks back and forth in a subconscious attempt to make himself look busy. It would be both lazy and wrong for him to merely wait for her to open the door.

None the less, he intolerantly waits as she squeezes her enormous body through the poorly lit hall. Declaring to himself that it would have been much faster to have opened the door through his own abilities he musters up the will to continue waiting. The lady is almost at hand and his lack of effort has all but received the reward.

The woman opens the door, and without waiting for her to pass, he pushes his way through. She looks at him but Colin is staring at the close-up of his feet again. She wants to speak with him about his behaviour but finds it difficult to start the conversation without the implied participation from his eye contact. From the past, Colin has learned that fewer people will disturb someone with their head to the ground. Though unaware of the glare of this particular lady he has avoided similar situations with the impolite trick.

Walking right past the staircase Colin travels to the far end of the hallway and stands in front of the elevator. The display is now, and has been for quite some time, fully incapacitated. Colin listens with great care for the sounds. There is a skill that he has developed. It is about knowing when the elevator is coming without the aid of the display to tell on which floor the elevator is sitting. He is fully prepared when it arrives and he calmly walks in.

It is a dark, scary elevator with a horrible smell of urine inside. Someone obviously could not hold his or her "number one". The light overhead flickers as if unsure whether or not to continue. The threat of confined darkness bothers Colin more than the rest of the people who use the elevator on a daily basis. The bigger issue for most, the smell, has been present for the entire time that Colin has inhabited the building. There is no stain to show where the mess originated. Somewhere in the building is someone who knows the answer. It may be only the culprit himself which would explain why he or she has not alerted anyone else.

Colin presses the button marked with a two and waits for the doors to close. The elevator lifts itself to the second floor with a thud. The cradle rocks as the doors open again. Colin saunters off and heads for his apartment. It is at the far end of the hallway just passed the stairwell leading up from the first floor. As he arrives at his door he steps back to double check the apartment address even though he has resided here for some time.

It has never happened but there is always the fear that he will gain entry into an apartment that is not his. Even though the story would sound great for the other street kids the crime of breaking and entering is one that should be committed with full intent.

Reaching forward, he slides his key into the latch. He mechanically turns it with one hand and twists the knob with the other. The door slips slightly agar. Colin rotates back to the original position then kicks the door open fully, skillfully using the force of the sliding door to free the key from the keyhole.

A crooked smirk on his face shows his pleasure. It is pleasure gained through the many skills that he has acquired like *that* skill that saves both time and energy. Colin enters the apartment and kicks the door forcefully against the wall behind it. The door ricochets off a rubber stopper with just enough momentum to close it once again without too much noise.

Surprised that there is nobody loafing around in the poor excuse of a living room he looks around for signs of life. He moves his head like a sprinkler, from side to side, almost confessing that he must have missed someone the first time through.

The apartment is empty but is somehow always a mess. It is empty in the sense that there are few items of furniture to occupy the room; not empty from a lack of people inside. There is a small red television on top of a brown microwave stand against a wall in the middle of the living room. Across from the television is a loveseat. A warm, flannel blanket must be used to hide the wear of the bench. There is a stand by the balcony with a cactus. The only other piece of furniture in the living room is a coffee table. The coffee table is extremely fine. It was there when Colin moved in and is an antique that was given to his roommate many years ago.

The microwave stand is missing one wheel and is level only because a group of magazines are shoved underneath. The magazines are purposefully arranged to make it difficult to see what types of magazines they are. They are the type more traditionally read by women and younger girls. It is a necessity for the apartment to use them, so they have been turned over, with the spines of the magazines facing the wall. By sitting in this position people are unable to read the titles of the magazines without resorting to much effort.

The television does not work properly and distorts the size of the actors' heads because there is something wrong with the picture tube. Adjacent to the television is the dead cactus, a miracle of nature. The cactus actually died from lack of moisture. Either out of respect for the dead cactus or in jest, a hat has been placed on one of the branches.

Around the corner from the living room is the dining room. In it are a couple of chairs. One of the chairs has been turned over. It has been upset for many days. In the corner is a patio table that doubles as a dining room table. Newspapers and empty beer bottles nearly cover it completely.

There is not much in the room yet it always looks to be in disarray. Two or three blankets lay draped across a few pairs of shoes and there are marshmallows everywhere. Typical for this sort of scene are the dirty dishes and music covers scattered about. There is a stack of mail still unopened ready to fall over an edge of the table. An old guitar is lying beside a four or five day old bowl of macaroni and cheese beneath the window.

Incidentally, the window is covered with a green garbage bag to keep out the sun. There is a curtain rack in place but no curtain. To save money from buying expensive material for curtains a friend bought Colin and his roommate a dark shower cover. Unfortunately, the shower cover is still sitting in the hallway closet, unused.

Colin kicks his shoes off and starts to walk down the hall towards his room. He hears someone freeing themselves from one of the bedrooms around the corner.

"Alright man, I will. Take it easy, okay?"

The person turns the corner and Colin quickly recognizes them as the neighbourhood drug dealer whose identity will remain anonymous.

"Hey, what's going on?"

The drug dealer is startled but covers the fright. It is not correct for the fashionable to be scared.

"Oh hey, Colin, I got some of that weed that you wanted. You got some cash?"

Colin does not say a word. He just takes out the money that he stole from Thomas. He also reaches into his other pocket and adds more money from before.

"Where did you get all *that* cash, man? I thought that you were broke."

Colin smiles. He does not speak right away. The delay is supposed to pique the interest of the drug dealer. Colin figures that he will be pressed for information and that the story will unfold. If a story needs embellishing it is more believable if the embellishment is not offered with ease. Unfortunately, the criminal loses interest in the question.

"I just got it, alright?"

Colin has a look of disappointment on his face. It is disappointment from his story going to waste but is seen differently by the drug dealer.

"Mommy and Daddy send it to you?"

Colin breaks in embarrassment but realizes quickly that opportunity has knocked a second time.

"No. I stole it."

He smiles too quickly to illustrate the desired casual behaviour. His inexperience shows which forces his listener to disbelieve the story.

"Oh right."

"I did."

"Anyways."

Colin offers the money and looks up to the drug dealer almost asking for approval. He no longer has the endurance to pry open the tale.

Snatching the cash in a swiping motion the miscreant reaches into a pocket for the goods. Pulling out a bag filled with many other little bags, Colin watches as curled lips replace the once stoic glance. Some of the bags have red and yellow pills. Other bags have pasty white tablets.

"Wrong bag."

The dealer replaces the first package into an inner pocket then pulls out another bag filled with little bags. These bags are either filled with fine white powder or have flaky grains of leafy substances. The dealer reaches in and pulls out one of the bags of marijuana.

Colin snaps his head back in protest to both the size of the bag and to the amount of marijuana within. His protest is obvious. In his opinion, the amount of money that he has offered the dealer should result in a larger quantity of narcotics.

The dealer fidgets with the bag wasting time. Colin is not the first in the recent times to object to the growing price of narcotics. In a voice quite apparently practised in solitude the criminal responds to the silent objection.

"Inflation my boy. Inflation."

After handing the bag to Colin the nameless hustler reseals the master bag then replaces it into the pocket from which it came. Without another word, and trying to keep from arguing, the dealer moves down the hall again. Colin follows while waving his arms in disgust and protest.

To tell you the truth Colin does not really enjoy doing drugs that much. Nor is Colin adamantly upset with the quantity that he received. His protest is more for show. Colin feels that by making a fuss he will keep up the image that he has worked so hard at attaining.

"Come on. I'm one of your best customers. You can't start screwing me around too."

The criminal pauses for a moment before answering, as if choosing the right words is important in this case. This is not a capital trial. It is not even a legal retail transaction. There is really no formal protocol for anything like this. Never the less, the words are carefully chosen.

"It is not *that* Colin. It is not about screwing anyone. It is all a matter of money. You know? It is simple economics. It is supply and demand, you know? I got something that you want, and I'm entitled to get a premium for taking the risk to supply you with it. As long as you are still willing to pay the amount that I am asking to supply you with it, we have a deal."

"What are you going to do with all that extra money? You're already living like royalty. You don't need any more money than you are already making. Don't be greedy. Seriously."

Still moving towards the exit the intimidating body turns to Colin to respond frankly.

"Everyone wants more money."

Colin is impressed. The response is difficult to negate. It is both concise and poignant.

"But seriously."

A fine argument from the mouth a genius. Colin finds himself wincing at his own retort. Fortunately, the plague to society is not interested in listening to Colin.

"The way I see it, Colin, the more money I make the larger the distance I can create between me and everyone else in this world. Then I won't have to deal with punks like you."

Colin may not be a genius but he is not stupid either. He can tell that there is some sincerity in the words. Obviously, it has a bite of sarcasm but Colin thinks that there is something more to the meaning.

People always look past blatant discussions. Colin has tried for many years to be subtle with his words but exact in his meanings. He has reached out as a confidante. He has cried out for assistance. All too often has he been disappointed because people have become illiterate to conversation.

Colin stops the dealer from leaving. He can be a great conversationalist when he wants to be and he believes that he may be on the cusp of intelligent dialogue.

"That's one way to look at it."

The door is now open and the dealer is almost out of the apartment. Essentially, the conversation could very easily be over. It is not.

"What do you mean?"

Colin can see interest in the face of his partner. Like a skilled fisherman ensuring that the marlin takes the bait Colin passionately speaks a single, motivating word.

"Money."

It works. Of course it works.

"Keep talking. You have my interest."

Colin speaks clearly as though his arguments have been calculated in advance.

"You say that it is a factor that frees you from areas of your life that you don't want to associate with."

"It can."

"I do agree. It can. Money can be liberating. It can be used to free you from something that you do not want to be involved in. It is also possible to say that the more money you make, the more things you can do to reunite yourself with your fellow man."

A glazed look crosses the face of the troublesome youth. Colin assumes that the idea is sinking in. Keeping with his frame of mind he continues with the next part of the argument.

"You see, it is money that brings together markets- which is to say, as you phrased it, both supply and demand. They work together. Therefore, I can only find what I need or what I want because the merchants across this land know before hand that I have money. It is

77

because of this knowledge that they are willing to offer their services. Their goods.

"By selling to a buyer, you complete the cycle. *You* create motivation for the cycle to continue. In a sense, *you* are what makes it impossible to break away from everyone. There is an implied participation.

"Money is what brings a buyer to you, and it is why you sell in the first place. If it is money that brings the people to you, how then can you turn around and break away from them after they pay you with money? You would be using the tool that created your bond to break your bond."

The dealer understands the argument. It is an interesting argument. Colin continues to finish his line of reasoning.

"Plus, the more money you have, the greater your ability to do for others. Not just to buy for others, but to help others. With money, you hold the power and the esteem of others. Money is what allows you to get things done. With money you become the keystone that holds the arch of the populace in tact."

"Well, whatever. No matter how you look at it, Colin, your prices have just gone up."

The one sided conversation is dead. Perhaps not just in this case either. Colin nudges the door allowing it to quietly close.

With the disappointment that his only chance at descent dialogue just walked out the door he again heads down the hall and into his room. After plopping down on the single mattress that he calls a bed he pulls his pillow up behind his head to get comfortable. To make himself even more snug he crosses one leg over the other. It is not that the new position actually feels any more comfortable but it would appear to anyone watching him that it is more comfortable. It seemed like the right thing to do at the time.

He reaches into the crack between the mattress and the wall and pulls out a small plastic bag of his own. It is a private cache of his marijuana. While adding his new purchase to the current amount, he revisits the conversation with the dealer. He thinks philosophically about the future of intelligent conversations in the world.

One of the defining characteristics of human existence is having the ability to communicate. It allows us to learn and to better ourselves. A recent trend, in the eyes of this troubled kid, is the bashing of this ability and the abandonment of the progress.

There is no doubt to the downfall of language. Few people fully learn the grammatical rules and even fewer people are interested in using them. As a people we invent words by abusing the regulations of our lexicon. We do not think about what we say and we are no longer judged through the meaning of our words. Correspondence alone lacks the formality of the past and it is slipping into abbreviated form. Convenience is becoming more important than is clarity.

Colin battles a fit of depression on this issue. Truthfully, Colin is very much for communication. He understands both the need and the benefit. However, in the past year or so he has developed disdain for language. The easiest way to communicate is through verbal language. However, the essence of language is not to communicate.

Language is supposed to sound right. It is a matter of poetry. It is elegant. It is supposed to invoke insight and thoughts. It is a catalyst.

In fact, the essence of language could be seen as the antithesis of the essence of communication. Language is a conduit used to convey cleverly worded ideas, often creating a stream of thought. Communication uses language to convey a concise, exact thought.

Colin wants to escape his depression over language and communication, and the future of a communicative society. He reaches into his bag and pulls out a joint. Though most of his cache is still in a leafy state, one pre-rolled joint still survives from a party from a few nights back. It is perfectly rolled with the ends wrapped tightly and neatly. It must have been rolled by someone other than Colin because he is not very good at that skill.

He stuffs the white object into his mouth in a fashion that resembles a particular actor from the nineteen fifties, and not the real actor himself, but one of the characters that the actor in question played in the movies. More correctly stated Colin stuffs the white object into his mouth in a fashion that he associates with a character portrayal of an actor from the nineteen fifties.

He pats his pant pockets in search of his lighter. His eyebrows crinkle while he strains to remember where he might have left the lighter. It is a painful day for Colin. He resorts without effort to a pack of matches sitting on his dresser rather than to fight his bad luck and his failing memory.

Even though the mattress sits a mere four and a half inches off of the ground he almost falls as he rolls off. Pulling himself up, off of the floor, he staggers over to the dresser to retrieve the matches. There is a faint knock at the apartment door. Colin lowers his head again out of habit. It is a conscious manoeuvre as he discloses his own social demise. Days like today take their toll on people like Colin. He finds himself crusading against mild depression.

Colin does not even flinch at answering the door. It is not for him and he knows that it is not for him. He grabs the matches and picks up a half filled ashtray from underneath a bunch of scattered papers beside his dresser.

Hearing his roommate Ian emerge from the depths of his own room to answer the door Colin slumbers back to his bed. The full weight of his melancholy looms over his body pressing it deeply into the single mattress. Colin feels the extra weight.

He leans his back against the wall and moves the pillow a couple of times, repositioning it to a more comfortable place. Ripping out a single match Colin strikes it coarsely against the back of the match cover. With a luminous spark the fire lights and Colin admires it with amazement. With the white stick in his mouth he brings the match to the tip and inhales deeply. His lungs fill, but not just with air. He inhales to capacity and captures the gases inside.

Colin glances and notices that the joint is burning under its own power so he flicks his hand to extinguish the match. With more care than is required he places it in the ashtray.

Colin has not yet experienced the typical psychedelic high of which drug users have become stereotypical. Being as self aware as he is Colin realizes that he has not yet experienced the typical high.

He often wonders if it would help but has not ever even wished that he could have the experience.

Understanding that his experiences are incomplete Colin always gives the same story when people ask him about doing drugs. He read the description that he gives once out of a book of short stories that chronicled the life of an old renaissance painter. Colin did not read the book entirely. He flipped through the pages and stumbled upon the passage.

His description always begins with numbness setting in from an overwhelming feeling of pins and needles. It is the feeling that is often visually associated with doing drugs or from being intoxicated. It is not necessarily associated with the type of drugs that Colin does but drugs none the less.

Next, he waves his arms frantically simulating the attack that the drugs make on the victim's mind. Colin does not explain that he is waving his arms for that reason. It is a symbolic gesture. He is fully aware of the symbolic gesture but his audience, most times, is not. He will go on to explain the ease and relaxation that takes control of his body.

Often accompanying this description are illogical psychedelic terms used by Colin for drama. He prefers to use terms such as "omniscience" or "mind blowing". The warping of time is an idea that Colin likes to have entered into the story as well. He will claim that the warping of time causes objects to move either more quickly or more slowly.

Drug tales and dreams are much like the study of fine wine. Each has a particular vernacular to which one must become familiar in order to fully appreciate the work. Along the same lines as the argument between language and communication, these fields of study can become foggy and unclear. The true meaning and exact terminology can be lost if one does not completely understand the verbiage.

Usually Colin will break his dictation to the audience at about this time. He leans back and puts his hands behind his head with a sour smile trying to make it look as though he is recalling a glorious high that he enjoyed to the fullest. After pausing shortly for more drama he whispers to the listener. He will not speak. It *must* be a whisper.

"Once you're lost in your mind, anything can happen."

To allow the listener time to run through his or her mind and imagine the feeling Colin will again pause and close his eyes. Gifted speakers always understand the importance of silence.

Finally, Colin will break the pensive state by adding an anecdote that is completely fictional. Colin tailors the anecdote to the listener. It is always something appealing with which the listener can associate.

Colin should have been a politician. He is good at tailoring situations to specific people. One of Colin's favourite anecdotes deals with a colourful flash of light that beams off of the walls in a cabin, and charges him with electrical energy.

It is difficult to remember exactly but Colin says he was at his friend's cottage. It was raining outside so he and his friend decided to get high. Colin never discloses what drugs he did at this cottage but the experience mirrors that of a mix of cocaine, acid, and marijuana all at the same time. The climax of the flashback is definitely the best part.

Colin remembers losing track of time. It becomes difficult to say if the sun was shining or if there were clouds covering the millions of tiny stars in the sky. The tale will change as well. One time it will be at night and another time will be during the afternoon.

While telling whichever version, Colin squints his eyes in disbelief continuing to explain how his blue sweater attacked him as he took it off. He describes how he grapples with the sweater for a long while. If the story seems to be going well Colin might even act out the battle. Then, with an excited rush as though he had just won the lottery, he interrupts himself. The senseless falsehood of how the walls started melting results.

He nods his head in amazement and describes to the listener the feeling of sitting in a large room out in the woods watching the walls drip down to the floor in front of your eyes. In great detail, he mentions the smell, the appearance, and the cross between both fright and anticipation that he received from the event.

The narrative slows as do all stories with their anti-climactic component. Colin and his friend decide to watch the little black and white television that they brought from home. He remarks to his friend that he can see the normally indiscernible television waves coming right through the walls, or what was left of the walls, and going straight into the set.

He exaggerates the humour of whatever episode was on the television at the time to give the impression that absolutely everything was comical. Like the budding politician he chooses the listener's favourite show so that the person can associate more easily with the incident.

Colin moves on to the lightning. He explains that in his heightened awareness of all that lay around him the lightning was a magical portrayal of Mother Nature's talent. The room simmers of noise as Colin waits for a timely intermission. Then, in a compassionate voice he again speaks to the listener.

"I swear to God I have never seen anything as fantastic as that one bolt of lightning though."

Every single time that he chronicles the account he says the exact same phrase, and always with a compassionate voice. Colin jiggles his head again waiting for the listener to ask himself or herself the inevitable question.

"What bolt of lightning?"

With a penetrating gape Colin hypnotizes the listener with his eyes before continuing. His mood is deliberate and his voice is balanced.

"Off, across the water I saw this enormous flash of lightning. Time almost stood still. I could see that flash of electrical energy for half a minute if not more. I focused on it, from back to front, and back again.

"I studied it so long and hard that the charge revealed itself to me. I would not say that we connected, but the viewing was more than incidental.

"I just watched and admired as the white light smashed into its smaller components. In an explosion of colour the flash of lightning burst into reds, blues, and greens. Every colour of the rainbow was present but the primary colours were vibrant.

"Colour filled the sky and I could watch single strips of colour disperse through the heavens. I followed some of the different colours as they raced towards the cabin. They came in through both the window and sliding door then bounced off of the walls and penetrated my body. It didn't hurt. It was exciting."

With the audience mentally picturing the scene Colin rests in unreserved stillness, desperately picturing anything else. He continually completes the story in the same way as well. There is always a time when he mentions that the high would wear off and that his body would feel as if he was falling from a great height. He would be falling yet he would be unable to look down. There would be the anticipation of crashing and hitting the proverbial bottom. Since he expects the pain so vividly and with such intense sensation he knows it will hurt and that the pain would eventually arrive.

Speaking as though he is an expert on the subject Colin claims that addicts live from one high to another high to avoid touchdown. He believes that if one is in control of the psychological journey, like he feels that he is, one could simply sleep away the worry. He sure makes the use of illegal narcotics sound tempting. Well-told and well-illustrated fiction can be quite persuasive.

Anyway, Colin hears the front door open after the long pause and he again inhales the smoke as the voices in the distance become louder. He holds the smoke in his lungs for an extended period of time, doing what his friends taught him to do, and he strains his ears to listen before he exhales with delight.

His door is closed and he cannot hear precisely what is being said in the other room. To the best of his knowledge Ian's brother is there for a visit and has brought with him some of his friends from college.

The faint voices become even more inaudible. Colin puts the joint back into his mouth for another puff. He makes note to himself of the increased perceived speed with which this particular smoke has burned.

Colin knows the layout of the apartment very well. In addition to this data he knows the personalities of both Ian and Ian's brother, Nick. He extrapolates this information attempting to diagram the activities materializing in the other room. Judging by the time of day he assumes that Ian's brother is merely passing time, perhaps waiting for a specific time of day before another event can commence.

Colin draws in more gases and rubs his temples to initiate supplementary thoughts. He tries to analyse his roommate in his mind to more scrupulously understand what sort of time delaying activity Ian might propose to his brother. Would he start to play some music or turn on the television? Both options seem too cliché for the enigmatic Ian.

The analysis is dramatically severed short. Colin hears more voices in the living room. Voices that he does *not* recognize.

Ian and his friends relocate to the balcony. The balcony runs along side both bedrooms. Finally, the day has brought Colin a stroke of luck. He can now hear the group more clearly from the partially open window above his head.

He quietly takes another drag and taps his smoke above the ashtray. Straightening his back in order to get a better listen he makes a conscious effort to be quiet. He does not want to mistakenly notify the others that he is listening.

His face starts to feel the numbness set in. He blows out forcefully but quietly and raises the corners of his lips. Colin becomes intently sensitive to his context. The voices from the balcony become as clear as day and the sweet, melodic babble of a woman echoes in his head. He giggles when he hears her speak.

"Whose dog is that out behind that yellow car?"

As though anybody really takes stock of which pets belong to whom in a city the size of this. Colin has to quell his laughter when another voice replies to his angel.

"I think that it belongs to that old man. The one in front of that shed. No, not him. Yes, *that* guy."

A good sign for society is that certain individuals still make the effort to familiarize themselves with the domesticated animals of others. The slender figure again places the narcotic into his mouth and grips it with his thumb and his forefinger to get a better look at how much of the joint remains. He figures that there is just enough left for one good puff so he brings it to his lips and sucks vehemently on the end.

Once more he holds the smoke deep inside his lungs and tosses the paper into the ashtray before it singes his fingers. Glancing down at the canister he notices that there is still some marijuana left. He does not have a clip that would facilitate him to finish the last section of the smoke. In his mind, he arranges to recover the modest amount of leafy substance later. After all, the price has increased and it does require more care and attention.

His vision fluctuates between blurry and sharp when Colin lifts himself up from his mattress. He inspects his space completely, doing so *not* in an attempt to locate an object, but to award him something with which to judge the flow of time. Once comfortable he moves towards the door.

All movement for Colin is functioning at a visibly slow velocity as he makes his way down the hallway from his bedroom. His chemically expanded mind conjures an image from an old television series about a man with bionic limbs. The look back in time instigates hysterical laughter. In a stern, serious voice he mimics the tone of the television series announcer from the beginning of the program.

"We have the technology. We have the knowledge. But more importantly, we have the drugs."

Colin collects his self-control and careens down the hallway into the living room. Forgetting his destination his first glimpse is into the kitchen. In plain view is the spaghetti stained white stove. It is a stove that has been neglected and overlooked by both Ian and Colin. They do not give the appliance any of the care or attention of which it deserves.

The stove is a marvel. Unbeknownst to either Ian or Colin the stove is perhaps the only stove ever to cook all recipes to the specified and allotted time. There is no guesswork needed when cooking with this stove. Unlike other appliances around the world this one in particular does not vary any results. Unfortunately the talent has gone, and will go unnoticed for some time.

Remembering the intentions for leaving his room, Colin stands watching the group on the patio before joining them. He steps through the patio door and onto the balcony with abundant impediment.

The group is intently listening as Ian is telling a story but Colin interrupts nevertheless.

"Hello everybody. My name is Colin, and I am Ian's roommate and most beloved confidante. How may I be of assistance?"

The attention of the crowd is stripped for only a short time. There are impressions of both confusion and disloyalty in the expressions of the guests. The mood snaps when a young woman lets out a funny, little, confirming laugh.

Colin scans the group to see who is present and looks first to Ian for security. After a quick pause on Ian, Colin moves his attention to Ian's right and recognizes Nick. This helps Colin to feel comfortable enough to continue. A grin forms on his bemused face. It is a lazy smile.

After delivering a nod in effort of greeting the quasi-friend, Colin maintains his scan of the field. The next face is one with whom he is not acquainted. Politely he raises the corners of his mouth rather than chance speaking without the grace of being spoken to. The suspension is brief and his head turns again to meet the next person. The ease of his actions drops noticeably. Colin knows, as he is altogether conscious of his surroundings that he will be able to identify none of the remaining visitors. The feeble smirk falls off of his face with the same intensity that it came. His stomach feels the discomposure of his embarrassment.

His mind takes advantage of the rush and play tricks. He starts to see things as though he is an adjacent part of the group. It is more than a feeling as though he does not belong. He does not sense being on the same level with them. He is neither superior nor inferior but is skewed from the common plane. It is as if he is watching himself and the others from a discrete vantage point. In his vision, though, he cannot see himself.

Ian stops his story and coldly introduces Colin to everyone except his brother. The omission is due to Colin having met Nick many times before. The group notices the indifferent almost callous manor with which Ian employs the introductions.

Colin clearly hears Ian speak but does not attempt to learn the names of the individuals to whom he is being introduced. Instead, he is busy staring at the mesmerizing young woman standing to the left of Ian. The same woman who laughed before. The same woman who also asked about the ownership of the local canine. She is his angel.

Ian completes the introductions and restarts his story. Colin does not pay attention though as he is still awe struck by the beauty of the woman who he has childishly named Juanita.

There is no logical explanation for her new name. She does not even appear to be of Spanish descent. Nobody on the patio has referred to her as Juanita and she has no pin or tag that addresses her *that* way. Colin simply failed to notice the angel's title in Ian's requisite introduction. Colin's gift to her of the name is to be taken with the heartfelt charity with which it was given.

In the distance, back inside the apartment, the telephone rings. Colin captures the eyes of his angel as she turns to see if Colin will respond. Ian is in the middle of his story. The appropriate action for Colin would be to answer the telephone. Juanita wonders if Colin understands his obligation as host.

Seductively, and with too much subtlety Colin flirts with Juanita by raising one side of his mouth. Ian flares as Colin again interrupts the story.

"Please excuse me as I tend to the pressing matter of the telephone."

Colin delays motion long enough to judge the impression he is leaving on the woman. Pleased by her smirk he goes back inside and scuttles to answer the telephone.

"Hello."

The squeaky voice of a receptionist on the other end replies.

"Good afternoon. This is the Kelsey, Lonette and Meyer law firm calling."

She pauses as if anticipating an exuberant reaction from Colin before continuing. There is no such reaction.

"I was wondering if I might be able to speak with a Mr. Colin..."

The training for Colin is certainly paying off as his flawless interruption completes another victory.

"Yes, this is Colin."

Unfortunately, there is no such smirk on the angel Juanita in close enough proximity to soften the mood of the receptionist. On the other end of the telephone the light figure rolls her eyes with disapproval of Colin's boorish behaviour.

Though playing to absolutely no audience she bobs her head from side to side. The bobbing of her head would not annoy Colin or anyone else claimed as a victim of the action even if he were able to see it. The intentions of the act however is to be offensive. The offence is only in her mind. She has not thought about her actions carefully or for long enough.

The act is made in jest of the conversation but truly combats the monotonous nature of her own job. Her ability to act immaturely while conducting a professional task only shows disrespect to her own vocation. Colin would not take offence to such an act but perhaps *she* should.

Colin is patiently waiting for her to continue. Holding back the sarcastic delight in her voice she continues with her duties by posing a question.

"Will you please hold as I connect you with your attorney?"

The two strangers are equally oblivious to the misrepresentations of good conversationalists that they are currently portraying. The receptionist had a strong argument against Colin as he interrupted her. She neither realized it in time nor spoke out against the infraction. Now she is committing another grave error in professional communication. She will not wait for the answer to the question that she has just asked.

The question is not rhetoric. It is also not the type of question that should be dismissed so quickly. There are many reasons that Colin may be either unwilling or unable to hold for the connection. Fortunately, Colin is fully prepared to wait.

What neither person will ever realize is that they may never again have as strong a possibility to engage in titillating conversation. Both Colin and the secretary are exceptional conversationalists when provoked. If they were to start the conversation over again and with a more serious tone it is likely that this information would reveal itself. A call such as this will not be an isolated incident as the law firm is obviously representing Colin. Another call similar to this one would most definitely result some time in the future, just as a similar telephone call was delivered to Colin yesterday.

The disappointing issue for anyone having this knowledge is also having the understanding that the information was always destined to be concealed. It is not an argument against freewill but a commentary on human existence.

In fact, the issue may be with the choices of both Colin and the secretary. It was a conscious decision for Colin to engage in narcotics today of all days. Today is definitely unique. Perhaps things would be different if he had chosen another activity or at the very least a better day.

"Okey Dokey."

There is a brief interlude. Colin has a chance to alter his mood and finds peculiarly soothing the melodic yet irritating instrumental version of a familiar hit song from the nineteen-eighties. A deep, resounding voice replaces the calming music on to the telephone.

"Hello, Colin?"

The question is a formality merely restating that the intended listener is Colin. It is a chance to recapture the attention of the dazed youth.

"Yes?"

Colin's question is truly a question. The melodic song from the eighties has stolen his short-term memory with some assistance from the marijuana of course. Colin forgot the reason that he was using the telephone. The question does not sound so silly to the recipient. In fact, the concise response gives the impression that Colin is ready to get to business.

"Hello there. This is your attorney."

"Dean."

Dean is surprised by the reply. His formal introduction usually acts as an icebreaker for business. The impression that Dean had of Colin was not flattering when they first met. After the initial meeting Dean commented to himself that Colin would have no retention for their next encounter. The first time that Colin saw his lawyer's full name was more than a month ago when a personal letter arrived for Colin requesting a meeting to discuss the case. There was also the call from yesterday.

"Yes."

Colin becomes aware of the astonishment in Dean's voice. It gives Colin a false sense of arrogance which instinctively forces him to stand up straight. He speaks with the authority that he could only have over the telephone and from a misdirected impression.

"What can I do for you Dean?"

Dean's eyes show his thoughts. They open widely and he asks himself if he has misjudged the youth on the other end of the telephone. The large amount of similarly aged clients that Dean represents typically lack the directness in speech of Colin. It is enough for Dean to forget the purposeful disrespect by Colin in his use of Dean's first name alone.

"Well Colin, I was wondering if it would be at all possible for you and me to blah blah?"

Of course Dean did not use the phrase "blah blah". Dean would never use such a phrase. Even if the phrase were appropriate Dean could not bring himself to sound so inappropriate. It is not in the nature that he has built for himself. The attention span of his audience is beginning to waiver.

It is impossible for Colin to understand Dean's request. In as polite a fashion as possible he asks Dean to repeat the question.

"I am terribly sorry Dean. There was a large noise in the background and I am afraid that I could not quite hear you. Would you mind repeating yourself?"

It is a pleasant request, phrased kindly. Dean does not mind.

"Absolutely. I was wondering if you had the time to briefly go over your case again, Colin. I should like to clear up any discrepancies that may arise under your testimony.

"As we discussed last time, I think that it is very important for you to testify in this case. The details of your situation need to be heard. It may be difficult, and could certainly work against us if not properly executed. This is why I think it important for us to meet again.

"According to my calendar your court appearance is coming up. Next Wednesday I believe."

"Do you want to bring it for me?"

Dean is dumbfounded. The illogical response causes a jolt in the conversation like one car hitting another in oncoming traffic. Dean refigures the words in his own mind. He attempts to change the order of the words to see if the statement could be rearranged, rendering it relevant. He even tries using synonyms to slightly alter some meanings but must admit to himself that the statement clearly does not make sense in the context. Ignoring the irrational retort Dean rephrases his earlier question.

"So when would you be able to come in and see me, Colin?"

The group on the balcony shares a laugh. It is an attraction hard to resist and Colin turns to see. Juanita smiles poetically to the group in clear view. Colin wonders about the good times that he is missing with the others. Did the same dog from before make another appearance? Perhaps Juanita was the one to bring about the roar of laughter.

"Hello?"

More time has elapsed than can be accounted for by the few thoughts of the juvenile. Colin snaps back to attention but is anxious and slightly disturbed about what he needs to do. He considers himself to have been taken completely by surprise.

A jolt of pain in his hand focuses his attention to the receiver that the particular hand is holding. Peering down at the telephone he is reminded of the conversation with which he is occupied. Desperately, he tries to recall where the dialogue ended. The intermission of words feels long. It feels as though it needs to be broken.

"Well that depends."

Colin chooses the reply because his memory gives him the impression that the last part posed to him was a question. The question was incomplete. Dean did use intonation on his single word-signifying a question; but the purpose of the intonation was to question Colin's participation and commitment at finishing the exchange. Dean's original impression of Colin starts to again take the place of the new impression. He decides to give Colin a last chance at redeeming himself as part of the conversation before taking over completely.

"Uh huh. And what exactly does it depend on, Colin?"

Colin giggles, still peering down at the telephone. His attempt to subtly orient himself with the conversation has failed and he knows.

It is something over which old friends would enjoy a laugh- being in the dark and trying to sneak back into the light without letting on that one is confused. Unfortunately, Dean and Colin are not friends. Dean could not allow himself a friend like Colin. It would not agree with the life that Dean has built.

"Have you ever really looked at the number five, Dean?"

Disenchanted with the direction of the conversation Dean answers before thinking.

"Pardon me?"

"Is it ever cool. It has everything that a single digit needs and more."

Dean leans back in his executive chair in his office across town. His face shows the stress of his discontent for his client.

"It has got a vertical line, a horizontal line, and a circular shape. Five is my new favourite number, Dean."

The latter part of Colin's statement bothers Dean the most. It can be seen as a sign of disrespect for a teenager to refer to his or her professional lawyer via the lawyer's first name alone. What bothers Dean even more is the use of his name at the end of the statement. It is something that Dean does quite often himself.

In law school Dean became friends with an elderly classmate. Dean respected the classmate and often modelled his own behaviour after the friend. One thing that stood out in the teachings was a lesson on effective communication. The wise student told Dean that an exceptional way to improve retention and participation from a listener was to include their name frequently in the dialogue. People seem to perk up when spoken to directly.

It vexes Dean that Colin is forcing participation and retention of such a silly fact. It is a fact that neither assists Dean in any way nor adds any information or closure to their problem. Colin's state of mind shows through to Dean.

Dean cannot fully comprehend how anyone can voluntarily abuse his or her physical and psychological being. He understands Colin better than Colin would be willing to admit. Dean is aware that Colin performs in an attempt to impress people who do not really matter in this world. At least people who do not matter to Dean.

With sharp words, Dean stops Colin from giggling himself to death.

"Colin, when you get a chance, can you blah blah blah?"

Still concentrating on the amazing number five Colin grunts to acknowledge hearing Dean. He does not hear what Dean is saying but he does hear him speak. The sounds are actually bothersome to his study of the amazing digit.

"Blah blah blah blah, blah blah, blah blah…"

The repetition of the sound in Colin's ear makes the omission of the meaning of the words obvious. It is enough to force Colin to question.

"What? You want me to what? What is going on?"

Dean has lost his patience. He speaks firmly and without compassion.

"Just call me tomorrow, okay? No. Wait. I will have my secretary call you and set up an appointment. Alright?"

The short, concise, fragmented speech is purposeful. Dean has had experience working with troubled youths and has had many comparable chats. Regardless to any agreement by Colin, the call will be placed tomorrow. Dean suspends his words for an appropriate time waiting for the information to sink in then says farewell.

He replaces the receiver onto the telephone on top of his thick, wooden desk and rubs his eyes in a stereotypical action that most people associate with job stress. It is the overly used action of movie producers and television crews that has become cliché.

Dean's hands remain over his eyes keeping out the light that has cunningly crept in from his office window. The fatigue and mental stress of his job allows him to pace back in time. Darkness fills his imagination and the images in his head become so vivid that you would swear that *you* could see them. He flashes back to his childhood.

Dean is the chameleon of the male species. He is the guy that you see all the time but who you cannot quite remember from where he is known. Dean is the type of guy who walked into class on the first day of school and voluntarily sat in one of the side rows near the back of the room. He did not sit there to be disregarded. He simply figured that if he were on an end row then he would really only have to deal with one neighbour trying to cheat, by looking at his test paper during examinations. The back of the class was always better for acoustics. Dean is cognitive to say the least.

He is the straight-backed, white toothed, average boy who always seemed a little above average. Dean is not thin and he is not hefty. However, when referring to him most people would say that he is either a little thinner or a little larger than the average man.

Dean is a forty-one year old whose heritage is primarily Italian though he was born and raised here. His demeanour is quiet and he is very well mannered by design. He is the one man who the C.I.A. would have trouble nailing down. His hair is sort of brownish-black. Definitely not blond, though it has light sections. His build varies from a little extra thin to a little more than plump depending on what is considered average at the time. His features have been described as distinctively average- whatever that means.

He loves his wife and would never cheat on her. He cherishes her need to present herself well and he truly does appreciate her. They have a happy marriage. It is not the pop cultural happy marriage with the two point five children playing in the backyard, and the dog lying in the sun on the deck. It is a real marriage. It is a marriage with real problems that the two work at solving together. They fall into and back out of lust regularly but always have a lifetime of love for one another. They may not turn heads as the cutest couple in the world; but they strengthen the formal institution of marriage instinctively and without effort. They make marriages around them better by association.

Appearances are important to Dean's wife and he helps her to keep them up as best he can. Their life together is content to say the least but probably looks better than average to everyone else because of Dean's involvement. This is something that they are unaware of but which aids in helping her to remain satisfied.

Dean's greatest aspiration is to raise the perfect child. Even though he wants to have children, Dean is a realist and appreciates the fact that it would be a miracle to have more than one perfect child. He is neither philosophical nor devoutly religious but he has heard arguments for monotheism as it applies to perfection.

Dean will be an exceptional father. He has worked at it for many years and is patient and diligent enough to put into practice the lessons that he has learned. Often, Dean will imagine full conversations between himself and his children-to-be. What they would say? How he would reply to their queries? When advising others on life's specific problems he will imagine himself facing the same turmoil. It helps to make him prepared.

He bases his answers on his belief system. Of course, when dealing with another person's problems there is less grey area. The problem can often be reduced to a black or white situation with a correct end-result. He is aware of the limitations of the exercise. The idea is to be more prepared for the future without falling into contradiction.

Preparation is the proverbial double-edged sword in this case. Dean is definitely more prepared than the average with respect to dealing with issues that may arise but he is definitely not ready to have children. For Dean to be the type of dad that he wants to be he will have to either be a father soon or create the wonder drug that would allow him to be as frisky as a kitten well into his sixties. His greatest aspiration of having the perfect child is clouded by many smaller battling aspirations with both work and home life. Since his background in pharmaceuticals is questionable at best, it would be beneficial for him to start his family now. Dean's wife is waiting to start a family. She does not have a preoccupation with financial security as does Dean.

Creeping into his subconscious is a place and time that often haunts him. He is a young child of about eight or nine, dressed in his Sunday clothes, sitting in the front row of a weather-beaten church. The lights are low and there is a soft harmony between the church organ and the gentle hum of the audience. The appearance is of an old scene from a television show set back in the sixties. The production values are low and there seems to be no colour.

A tension is in the air but it is unusually dense for the imagination of an eight year old.

Dean looks up to the long hanging lights and his attention casts to the beautifully stain-glassed window beside the pews. He knows that it is early afternoon but cannot imagine why the bright sun and all of its power cannot penetrate the mystical glass and fill this bleak room with an explosive eruption of colour.

Dean turns his head forward again then looks deeply into his lap while biting his lip. He hears the rustling of the crowd while they take their seats. As the minister commences speaking young Dean battles the urge to look up.

Dean normally pays close attention in church. He is not particularly religious but is disciplined. Today his mind is elsewhere.

He cannot exactly explain why but Dean suddenly feels a need to twist his body and swing his arms in frustration, but he does not. He simply sits still nibbling his lip completely motionless. Dean's hands begin to sweat abundantly and his left leg starts shaking uncontrollably.

Like a lion getting ready to pounce, Dean prepares his mental state gaining enough momentum to raise his head. Just before the adjustment he closes his eyes. It is a well thought out decision used to move his eyes into a specific position without much hassle. With a stoic glare and pursed lips his head sits in a level position.

Opening the right eye first to check if the coast is clear he pauses before continuing. Then, all at once, Dean throws open both eyes as wide as they will go. His head shifts slightly while locating the target and a small layer of tears form under his lids. Looking through the blurred vision of his moist eyes Dean focuses on an open casket.

Even though he cannot see her now, the impression of his mother's face lying on top of the silky white pillow in the casket is burnt into the back of his mind. The minister's words, the people around him and everything else in the church at that moment seem to bleed away without form. The lack of light from the sun outside joins the darkness. Time goes quiet.

With a shake of his head Dean is brought back into the reality of present day. He exhales a large gust of stagnant breath and pretends to himself that everything has returned to normal. Anger *has* filled his soul once more.

He mumbles in a tone that no audience could hear something about his client Colin being an immature bastard. The anger is trying to get out. It unfortunately did not escape with the stagnant breath from before.

Dean is not thinking about Colin at all. Nor is Dean mad at his mother. This is simply not the case. Dean did not wallow in the misery associated with losing a parent at a young age. Perhaps if he had the anger would have left his body earlier.

Dean's disposition with respect to his mother's death is admirable to some. He will even thank her spirit when something good comes from an act that he considers to have accomplished on his own. It is a tribute to her from him and shows that strength can come from pain.

Dean was very young when his mother died and his father did not take the loss well. Many times, Dean has thought about his father's reaction. Scientifically speaking there is a finite number of people who have ever dealt with the loss of a loved one. Even if everyone on earth for all time has dealt with a similar situation, there is still a finite number. This means that it would be possible for one to rank, in order, the reactions of all people into a scale. Dean has thought many times about the reaction of his father to his mother's passing. Many times has he wondered about the position of this reaction on the continuum.

Fathers are supposed to be strong. As a parent they should be the crutch onto which the grieving children can lean. Would this fact greatly lower his father's ranking?

One Christmas a few years ago Dean thought about the reaction deep into the night. His wife was asleep in bed already and his father was laying in a recliner. Dean uttered a statement; though he doubted the validity from the very moment that he manipulated his lips to form the first word.

"You may have been the saddest person to ever fake being strong."

Even though he did not want to Dean had to grow up a little soon after his mother's death and start doing things for himself. He had to grow up for his father. He had to do things for his father.

His father had always been a good supplier for the family. They were not rich by what society deems wealthy but the family problems were not financial. Their financial stability did not really appeal to Dean, though.

Stability was something that somebody else could take away without very much trouble. Dean wanted to be secure. Truly secure. Dean wanted to be wealthy.

To Dean, money means happiness and power. It is not overbearing happiness or power. It is not the type of happiness or power which would make successful one's life. However, it is the sort of happiness that leads to different types of happiness- truer happiness. It is the type of power that allows for further benefit from some other sort of joy. It was then and there that Dean decided to become a lawyer. Money was to take the place of the security that a little child feels when nuzzled in his mother's bosom.

Dean did not blame his mother for leaving him because he figured that it really was not up to her and that there was no decision for her to make. Deep down Dean knew that if she had the choice she would have been with him always. Life is such that there are always things beyond your control. Success if often considered being what one accomplishes within the scope of their control; while fortune is considered that which one experiences outside of the same capacity.

He thanks his mother's spirit because he believes that the independent strength that he has acquired branches out from learning a discipline and a work ethic at an early age. Responsibility and dependability are traits about himself that he always admired. Both of these traits needed to be heightened to deal with her tragic departure.

He did accomplish a lot on his own. Dean worked very hard and successfully completed law school through his own volition though graduating only in the top quarter of his class. Law school was difficult, especially for Dean. He was not competing against a fictitious group either, like the hero or heroine of a short story. These were real people all with similar dreams and similar motivations.

Dean has also found himself a wonderful wife. It sounds cliché to phrase it in such a fashion but she really was found in the truest sense of the verb. He searched for a specific person in his mind- not defined by deoxyribonucleic acid or chromosomes; but rather, character traits and personality. She was exactly *that* person.

Together, they have created a wonderfully warm home. This achievement may not sound like much at first but it really is something of which to be proud. Dean's good fortune and hard work is what many people would consider valid success. Valid success is regard by those who define it as being true success. It is better than regular success because the term has become very subjective. Valid success combines both luck and effort. It is possibly the toughest triumph to achieve.

The death of Dean's mother is not the fault of his father. Children can sometimes unwittingly place blame on a surviving parent for the passing of the other parent. Dean is not one of these children. There are a lot of emotions that Dean has for his father but neither anger nor blame are one of them.

There was a point when Dean pitied his father. It was a brief, passing moment. Both time and the experience of being married himself have allowed Dean to understand his father's suffering more completely. Pity is the last thing for his dad that Dean now feels. The two of them are not as close as they once were. The distance between them gaped the day Dean visited home and found the old ring.

It was a month before Dean finished his first year of university while attaining his undergraduate degree. He was returning home for a short break before starting his final examinations. The time was cautious for Dean but the return home brought a comforting joy.

Quiet and empty was the familiar house. No alarming calm that is typical of a second rate horror film but a realistic break in a passive moment. A realistic break in a reflective moment. Dean's father was still at work so to both pass the time and avoid reflection Dean began looking in the drawers of the furniture in the living room.

Specifically, he was looking in the living room. This is not to be confused with the family room. Dean was happy to be home but did not want to give the impression that he was too comfortable. The living room was a more formal setting where guests would normally be entertained. Dean wanted to be seen as a guest.

For about an hour and a half Dean searched until he finally found the item for which he had not consciously been looking. There was a flimsy wooden case that looked to be a miniaturized version of a pirate's chest hidden deep in the innards of the furniture. The discovery of the item would intrigue any who found the article. It certainly did with Dean.

He took the chest into the less formal setting of the kitchen. Stopping only to pour a glass of orange juice the varsity scholar opened the chest with the passion of a buccaneer on the beach of a tropical, uncharted island.

The ring that he found inside was a tarnished school ring from many years ago. Immediately, it inspired thought. There was a conversation reciting itself in Dean's memory of the time when he first received the bauble.

The history of the band is riddled with forgotten tales. It belonged originally to Dean's grandfather. The family was sceptical about his grandfather ever actually attending the school in question. Many versions of possibilities were explained to Dean when he was a child none of which he could remember that day. Dean did not get the chance to know his grandfather but truthfully would have never asked about the ring even if he had.

Curiously, the band was not passed down through Dean's father but instead it was forwarded along through Dean's mother. This is interesting because the ring did not pass through blood relations. Another forgotten legend about the ring was that Dean's grandfather gave it to Dean's mother when she was merely dating Dean's father. Most family members remember it as if the delivery was either at the wedding or soon there after. Nobody ever knew how important *that* act became to the lineage of Dean's bloodline.

His parents had been dating for some time but without much attachment. Neither had been very popular during their formative years. They would attend gatherings together because they enjoyed similar activities. After a few years of this sort of coincidence they began dating exclusively. This was not a big deal for either of them because there was really no competition with which to contend. She began wondering about her future. He did not.

They were together the night that Dean's grandfather passed along the ring. Dean's mother had been seriously questioning the connection but without actually making any inquiries. Her thoughts were intentionally interrupted by the gift.

When first accepting the loop she did not think of it with appreciation. It was when her future father-in-law explained his rationale that the message struck. Never able to confirm her belief, the gift became a response to her thoughts. In essence, the answer was given to the questions that she did not ask.

A sacred heirloom was being offered to her so that in the future she could pass it along to their child. She never spoke about the night to anyone. It did however give to her an immediate sense of belonging and acceptance by the family. *That* night alone set her mind about the future. She was successfully swayed by providence.

It was behind moist eyes that she handed it to Dean many years later.

The sentiment was unfortunately exercised too early. Dean did not have enough emotion within himself to accept such a gift. Beyond that, the ring was far too large in circumference for his tiny finger. He began by wearing it around his neck on his favourite chain. The same chain that broke a week and a half later when it got caught on the handlebars of his bicycle.

The chest that Dean examined on the break before his final examinations was also full of trinkets that belonged to his mother. Dean would pick up an ornament and thoughtfully examine it before setting each item back down on the kitchen table. The ring sat on the second finger of his right hand as he looked through the items of his late mother but it did not rest properly. The ring was positioned so that it rested in the middle section of his finger.

Instinctively, the box felt empty. Doubting his judgment he looked inside to be sure that there was nothing left to examine. With serendipity he stumbled upon one last piece. The only thing remaining inside was an old note on paper that had turned a bland yellow. It was a prize that most would have left a mystery. It even looked irrelevant. It was short and informal. Due to the juxtaposition of an insignificant piece amidst priceless sentimental artefacts Dean felt compelled to finish. The note was simple but would alter Dean for the rest of his life. Two hundred and thirty-six words printed by his mother and written for his father.

A little more than four pages long, the note had been scribed shortly after Dean's birth. There are only three people in the history of the world who know the contents of *that* letter. Immediately after reading the note Dean ripped it into little pieces and burnt every last fibre until there was nothing remaining but the faded, haunting memory.

The letter contained an apology. She wrote about her regret and her sincere sorrow for minor transgressions that had passed. Dean was upset not by the content but for another reason.

The note addressed in minor detail an issue of Dean's father. He had not cheated on his wife or murdered an old lover. It was nothing that exotic. In Dean's opinion however this particular matter was much worse.

The financial stability of their family was aided by the high wages of the factory where Dean's father worked. An issue was addressed about promotions at the factory that had been offered but rejected. They were rejected by Dean's father on several occasions. The promotions would have yielded more money and allowed better hours. More importantly they would pull the aging worker off of the line and gently settle him into an office. It was on the factory floor that his father's hearing was damaged. The promotions would have meant a better working condition in addition to both a better life style and esteem.

It must be mentioned that Deans' father is from Italy. He came here when he was very little and his formal education is limited. He is not an ignorant man but he never really learned to read very well. He lacks any external validation of education through formal certification.

Rummaging through the local newspaper or finding something to watch in the television guide is fine but lengthy long-winded technical applications written in legal terminology becomes frustrating. Some of the documents drafting the promotion proposals were over ten pages in length. Dean's father did not want the hassle of completing them. There was also the issue of pride. Retention and understanding would be challenged.

Even now, this situation causes problems for Dean yet the source of the problem is still unclear. He was not enraged with hatred of his father simply because he allowed the additional remuneration to pass. His father had always been a good provider. It is also not the case that he pitied his dad for not having the ability to read ten technical pages. Dean has seen his father rise above many crises. It is not embarrassment, nor disdain, nor humility.

An interesting revelation for Dean is that his father is considered by many to have achieved valid success. Perhaps this knowledge is the enemy. Maybe it is not that the family could have enjoyed a slightly more liquid financial freedom. The issue may not be the size of their house or the age of their car. The failing health could be attributed to many factors other than work environment. It could be, perhaps, that it is not the height of the bar over which his father had successfully leaped. Maybe it was the knowledge that the bar could have been just a little bit higher. Even valid success can be proven invalid.

Anyway, Dean paces around his office for a while until he can calm himself down. It is within his control. Then he wipes his palms signifying that it is time to return to work.

Using the stylish black pen with the gold lettering he inscribes a question mark in the column of his daily planner as a reminder. Tomorrow he will need to contact Colin in order to arrange a meeting. The court appearance is drawing near and they need to be prepared. He closes his book after checking his watch first. Dean pushes the book up into the left corner of his desk to the correct resting place. He pauses for a second and then checks his watch again out of habit.

This routine disturbs Dean even though it is a situation of which nobody else is aware. He often catches himself referencing his watch, pausing then examining it again less than a minute later. It is as though the world continued to move at the speed of life for a brief moment while he was caught in a rift. Though unaware of the effect that the rift would have on the outside world he is aware of the rift and is obligated to mark the occasion diligently by noting the time.

What bothers him even more is when he is asked the time shortly after having checked his watch. The question mandates that he examines the timepiece anyway. Even worse is that he is forced into the rift. It bothers him when his own wits fail him but bothers him more when his hand is forced.

Looking around the room as if hoping to find something to do Dean turns his head and tries to crack his neck. He gathers some papers on top of his desk and bangs them down, bringing them together homogeneously one on top of the others.

Dean is startled by the sudden ring of the telephone. He sits perfectly motionless until it sounds again, for no good reason, before answering.

"Hello?"

After a short time Dean repeats the greeting. The person must have not replied.

"Hello?"

There is a pause sufficient enough to presume a reply from the other end. Dean's voice changes signifying that he recognizes the voice.

"Oh. Hi there. What a surprise. What are you doing calling me here at this hour?"

An appropriate stillness fills Dean's office as he allows the person on the other end enough time to answer the insignificant question.

"Oh. Alright. I suppose that *that* could be arranged. I cannot quite speak for everyone else but I would love to. You know, I cannot even remember the last time that we all did that."

As though the other players on stage in a play take their cue, the sounds of regular life fill the void of words. Dean nods his head and laughs along as if seen by the other person when their conversation becomes more personal. Settling into a more relaxed state Dean allows his metamorphosis into a less professional appearance. He is conscious of the fact that nobody else is in the room.

"Do you really think that we could get away with that?"

Dean laughs hysterically. It is the type of laugh that starts out heavy and builds with intermittent breaks between breaths. It ends in a thorough cough.

"Yes. Yes."

There is a shared social obligation to contribute nonsensical utterances at a high velocity when sharing an inside joke with a friend over the telephone. Dean would never cross the grain of socially accepted behaviour.

The two friends continue discussing the humorous piece of history for a few minutes. Dean does little to provoke the subject but also does little to quash it.

The laughter subsides and his tone again becomes direct.

"So when would you be leaving?"

For anyone who was listening, the question would seem out of place.

Once we, as a species, begin to speak we start to learn and to teach ourselves the rules of conversing. There is a philosophy behind true conversation. We need to learn and to abide by the necessary give and take approach that is essential when exchanging ideas.

If the approach to this exchange is not correct there develops a gap in continuity. Changing subjects dramatically is one example. Conversations with this gap sound choppy and distorted. Continuity of conversation is like a decibel level for noise. There is a certain range, within which the setting can sound normal. Above or below that range there is distortion. Activity can continue but only with a price.

Dean's question would sound distorted to anyone who was listening. It seemed like a large jump in topics and did not sound as though it had a proper lead, in which to follow. The attack on communication to which Colin opposes is weakened by both friendships and emotional bonds.

Part of all communication is mental. This fact enables friends or people with strong emotional bonds, such as sisters, to increase or decrease substantially the socially accepted gap in conversations. Knowledge of how one thinks or of what one is thinking can speed up or slow down a conversation to a comfortable level outside of the normally accepted range. The price is that the conversation becomes comfortable for only those people with the esoteric information. Perhaps something like that is happening now.

Dean leans back in his chair to comfort himself as he listens to the answer. A raised pitch in his voice suggests an attempt to interject.

"As far as I know, you see, we would already be there. In that case, you wouldn't have to do anything except come straight in, right?"

Dean unconsciously rubs the back of his head with his hand. It is some time before he speaks again.

"Well why don't you lie to him and say that you'll be staying with your mother for a while?"

He playfully brushes his hair upwards in disagreement with the natural path of the follicles then replaces the hair with a single, smooth, downward stroke.

"And when you get there the first thing I want you to do is to come to my room and have a drink with me. Then, if you play your cards right I might take you out for dinner, a movie and who knows what."

The muscles in Dean's cheeks pull at the corners of his lips and he nods his head to no audience. Before chuckling, he again interrupts the other person.

"Down in the lobby I suppose."

Though not a hilarious punch line, the simple phrase invokes laughter at both ends. Dean brings his finger to his eyes checking for tears of laughter but there are none. He exhales a joyous sigh.

"Whew! Anyways, what are you going to do with Nick then, because he is too old to do something like that isn't he?"

Leaning forward again in his chair Dean sounds stunned with the response that he receives.

"Isn't he older than that? I could have sworn that he was."

It has been a long conversation already. Dean is not a great conversationalist, especially over the telephone. The lamp on top of his desk captures his attention and focus. Though, he manages well to remain in the conversation.

"Oh well then, I guess it *won't* be a problem."

His interest has waned. Fortunately, there is a break in the conversation that is longer than the socially accepted amount of time.

"Well I suppose that I should let you go, but thank you so much for the telephone call."

He quickly switches the hand with which he is holding the receiver so as to not miss a word, and tries again to crack his neck. Again, the lamp becomes the target of his eyes for no important rationale. Dean becomes aware that he is focussing on the lamp and it troubles him briefly.

His face turns a terrible shade of disbelief and his jaw makes a final drop while he listens to the voice on the other end of the telephone.

"I can't believe that. Are you sure?"

Putting his hand to his mouth in an attempt to cover his awe, Dean initiates the shaking of his head.

"You know, I would have never guessed that she would be that type of girl."

Dean's personal secretary knocks politely on the door then impolitely enters his office while still unwelcome. It would normally be acceptable for her to enter after the rhetoric knock due to the professionalism of the office. However, today is completely divergent from regularity. This is something of which neither of them might yet be aware.

While maintaining a deep interest in the telephone conversation Dean looks to her and quietly asks what she needs. Instinctively, his manor again becomes professional and confident. Before she can answer Dean puts the mouthpiece of the receiver back in front of his mouth.

"Uh huh."

The gesture is used to fool the person on the other end of the telephone into thinking that Dean is still devoted to their cause. He again moves the mouthpiece away from his mouth and beckons a response from his secretary without a word. The apathetically loyal assistant whispers her message.

"Officer Oysone phoned and wants you to transfer his Thursday appointment to next Monday at eight-thirty in the morning. I checked your schedule, and validated the transfer, but I just wanted to check with you."

Dean speaks briefly into the mouthpiece.

"Who in their right mind puts that much into one of those little mugs? I think she should get her head examined."

Taking his appointment book from the top left side of his desk Dean opens it to the date in question. He fingers down the page until he sees the timeslot for eight-thirty to verify that he is free. There is a blank space beside the time which indicates a vacancy so Dean raises his thumb to give the signal to his assistant. She raises her eyebrows in response and turns to leave. With her back towards Dean she crosses her eyes and raises her thumb indicating with exaggerated sarcasm that she is upset with his unprofessional response to her concern. Dean is bothered by his unusual approach as well but is unaware of the effect on his loyal associate.

"You've got to be kidding me."

Dean closes his appointment book and returns it to the resting spot once more. He makes a puzzled gesture with his eyebrows.

"Oh. Okay then, but you have to promise to call me soon and finish the story."

He quickly glances at his watch to see how late it has become. It would have been a great time for a rift.

"Well, I suppose that we will see you soon. And…"

It is obvious that Dean is interrupted. Another story has undoubtedly started to unfurl because Dean again sits back in his chair.

"No, I don't think that we need any."

The lamp has competition for Dean's attention. It is a visual distraction grappling with an audible disruption. Through the vent in the wall on the opposite side of his office Dean can hear a faint whistling sound.

"You just tell her to come and talk to me. I'll set her straight, alright?"

The whistling wins the battle. Dean strains to hear it more clearly.

"We already have a black pot though. The hubcap was painted long ago and if she really wants the pot then she can call the paper mill herself."

There is a chance in the conversation for Dean to escape for a short period. The voice on the other end has started a long passage. The timely break allows Dean the opportunity to revisit his past once more.

The whistling through the vent is a catalyst. It reminds him of his thirteenth birthday. Dean was not very close with many of his cousins from Italy but had an outstanding week when Dean turned thirteen with one of his cousins who was about his age. The two near strangers had a discovery worthy of note which Dean has never forgotten. The discovery dealt with whistling.

Dean's cousin started to whistle a tune while they were walking to the store. The refrain sounded familiar to Dean. He listened to the melody with great consideration and at one point he whistled along, thinking that he knew the song. The tune that his cousin whistled was a religious hymn from Italy that Dean had never heard.

The discovery materialized the very moment that Dean began whistling. His cousin had to stop. Dean wanted him to continue, thinking that the two of them would harmonize in unison, but his cousin could not. There was something that imposed a stop to the blowing.

It is very rare, if ever, that one would hear duelling tunes being whistled within earshot of one another without a specific purpose. It is the same phenomenon that creates difficulty when attempting to recall the melody of one song while listening to another.

The two blood relatives spent the day looking for people who were whistling happily. When they would find someone engaged in the activity they would stroll nearer and whistle a song themselves as a test. Each time, the other people were made to halt by the mystical force.

Dean has to abandon his flashback to rejoin the dialogue.

"I saw at least two or three pennies scattered carelessly on the floor, but her bottle of water was right were she left it. On the night stand."

Dean again checks his watch.

"It is getting late. Maybe we should just leave this for another day?"

He stares motionless for a moment before shaking his head, visually contesting what his companion had just said.

"I don't really want to argue with you about it. It will all work out anyways."

A vision of glee overtakes his face as he anticipates the end of the chat.

"Alright, we will see you then. Good-bye."

The telephone receiver is placed gently on the hook. Dean grumbles under his breath about the length of the call. Though he has strong ties to the person with whom he was speaking Dean admits that they were too hard to get out of the discussion.

Dean is being hypocritical but does not know it. He has some really annoying conversational habits. The most annoying tradition is that he is the type of guy who is always starting discussions too late. One would not notice as distinctly if he or she had the time in which to finish the conversation but if you are going one place and Dean is heading somewhere else along the same route then Dean is not the person with whom you want to be walking.

In particular, this becomes evident for those co-workers who walk with Dean from across the street where they park. He often lets the awkward lags and silences in pleasant morning routine build until they are just about ready to bludgeon themselves unconscious in order to escape the grasps of the idle repartee.

Dean is an individual who is quite in tune with his surroundings to an even greater extent than the average person. Typically, Dean will stumble upon a question or topic of great interest to his walking companion that would ignite a very titillating conversation. A conversation that they would not be easily willing to leave.

Dean usually enjoys his elevator ride each morning. There is quite often a topic of discussion that is of interest to both Dean and the other person. The problem is that Dean's office is just off of the elevator. Not knowing this, the other participant is often taken by surprise by the abrupt completion or expected completion to the mixing of words.

Dean's regular move is to stand in the doorway of his office leaning outside just enough to hear the other's voice. He will often appear disturbed that a stranger, who is peddling himself or herself backwards while quickly paraphrasing an intelligent thought in order to release it in time to the universe, cannot read the signs of a proposed ending to a discussion.

This has been debated by many people in the building. Since it has happened on numerous occasions and to various people it was inevitable that two of these people would share their experience. Dean has been labelled for his annoying tradition.

It is difficult to decide which of the two following situations is worse: Is it more disturbing to be unaware of another person's criticism? Or is it more detrimental to have complete knowledge that you are a negative anecdote for someone else?

The first would most definitely result in pity. At some point, someone will exact judgement on you for something about which you are unaware. It is likely out of your control. It would be even worse to be in a situation where you could easily explain your actions. It might be possible to either defend yourself entirely or at least discontinue the negative action in question. It is sad for anyone to think that people could hold a disapproving opinion that could be corrected without great difficulty.

The second condition is undeniably a common fear. Anecdotes are typically humorous or unique. They are about situations that do not arise commonly. It is a common concern for something about us or about something that we have done to be brought up on many different occasions. It becomes humiliating. To have the knowledge, not only that people are aware of our unique feature or negative action, but that they will spread word to others in the future can be crippling.

Friends of Dean have become comfortable with the idea of saying their intimate words of parting across the many meters of land that can separate them. It is all part of knowing Dean. He is always doing *that* sort of thing.

Anyway, Dean's secretary gently raps on the door again and walks in which breaks his train of thought. He is thinking about his friend with whom he just finished conversing. It had been some time since last they spoke and Dean was wondering about how quickly life can change. He is disappointed that they spent so much time talking without really delving into the mundane daily activities that truly shape one's existence.

His attention is immediately thrown to her though she does not wait for his acknowledgment before starting.

"Your last appointment of the day just called, and cancelled. Mr. Quonair said to make sure that I apologized to you in person, and wanted to reschedule for sometime next week. I told him to call back on Monday to set up another appointment, and he said that he would."

"Did Peter say why he couldn't make it?"

"I'm afraid not. But he was rather insistent that I apologize to you immediately."

She really wants for Dean to recognize Peter Quonair's insistence. Scheduled meetings are often disturbed due to immediate circumstances in either participant's life. It is a common occurrence. It struck her as odd that the gentleman asked her repeatedly to express his regret for the minor breach. She wants for Dean to recognize this but he does not.

Dean sits motionless, again, as she departs through the door. It is as though he is watching for something more to happen. He is experiencing the anticipatory state that one achieves when lead down a scripted path. The same state that one enters when watching a vaudeville performance or a properly acted scene in a class for acting lessons. He has a feeling that something more should happen, but of course nothing does.

With nothing else to do he jumps up and gathers some of his necessary papers. He reaches behind the chair and grabs his briefcase then places it on the desk in front of him to open it. The stack of papers from before is deposited inside. Opening one of the desk drawers Dean collects some personal items also for the briefcase. He inspects the time once more while putting his wallet into his pant pocket.

With all of the necessary items needed for his exodus already in the case, Dean closes it softly which locks it securely. He walks to the door and turns the lights out by flicking the switch on the wall. The dropping sun still busts through the window to the outside leaving the room only a little more dimly lit. A moment of shame arrives with nobody around to enjoy it. Dean turns the elegant handle of his office door and pulls at the same time to open it. Though the door is not locked the friction of the metal in the door frame forbids it from opening. Dean laughs about his feeble attempt and rests the door for a second attempt. It was only a mental error. He just needs to focus. Learning from his mistake Dean turns the handle, pauses almost too long then pulls it open without fail. As he enters the main reception area he notices his assistant turn to him and wonders if she is privy to the minor failure from a moment ago.

"Have a good night tonight. I'll see you tomorrow."

He smiles to her as he passes.

"Thank you. Bye now."

There is nothing in her response with which to determine whether or not she knows about his trouble. Still needing to exit through the main door Dean ensures success by pausing again after twisting the knob. There is no friction this time. It is a flawless finish to his departure. Dean walks out of the office with a beam of victory. His reward is the most precious reward of all- time. There is someone standing in front of the elevator who has already pushed the button to summon it. With a glance at the numbers on top of the door Dean realizes that he has little time to wait.

"Good afternoon."

"Hello."

The elevator arrives and the doors open smoothly. Being the gentleman that he is, Dean allows the elderly man to board first. As Dean walks onto the elevator he turns to the number board. He pushes the button marked for the lobby then spins to the aging figure.

"Are you going to the lobby too?"

The old man smiles so Dean assumes that his assumption was correct. His arms fall to his sides with the briefcase held firmly in his left hand. As good form predicts the two stand side by side staring blankly at the digits above the elevator door in silence. There is strain on the old man's face. It is strain caused by mental excitement. He is thinking hard about something and is working figures in his head. Dean too is thinking. The ride home can be a long one, depending on the traffic pattern, and Dean wonders if he should use the facilities on the ground floor before exiting.

Some people are very good at gauging the length of time that they will require before again using the washroom. Dean is not one of these people. There is an inconsistency in Dean's diet that hinders him from gaining the data necessary to calibrate the gauge. There are many days on which Dean will miss meals due to the time constraints set by his work schedule. Other days, he may eat once and then be forced to eat again because of a business meeting. The size of his meals can vary dramatically along with an almost daily changing hydration level.

Another problem that this causes is a misunderstanding of his hunger. Hunger is actually a physical quality. It is a state in which the body rests. Hunger causes physical conditions. For Dean, however, hunger is a mental issue. Similarly to western culture, hunger for Dean is based in large part on time. Rather than being lunch time because he is hungry Dean becomes hungry because it is lunch time.

He also considers noises from his belly as a sign that he is hungry. This is actually only a sign of emptiness in his stomach and a build up of gases due to the stomach acid passing through his intestines. His stomach does not speak to Dean if he neglects food for a while. Dean does not suffer from the physical conditions of hunger and could probably not recognize true hunger even if it was presented to him. There are no sharp pains nor does he acquire a head ache. If he becomes aware, however, to the extent of time that has elapsed between meals he can become relatively hungry.

About halfway through the ride to the lobby Dean looks to the old man.

"Wouldn't you say that it has been a lovely day for this time of year?"

The old man replies out of obligation, still working the figures in his head.

"Why yes, it has been good. Warm. Yes."

Dean nods his head. He is a very visual specimen.

"Did you know that the warmth of the sun at this time of year is crucial to seniors? It actually helps their blood system which in turn helps their immune system."

Dean recently watched a television program on the subject. The old man loses his train of thought for a couple of reasons. Most people would choose their words more carefully and may not have referred to the man as a senior, having just met. The old man does not object but is taken by the approach. It is almost refreshing. Also, the old man has a growing concern for his immune system.

"Is that right? You know, I really need to..."

The sharp beep of the elevator sounds indicating that it has reached the lobby floor. It is loud enough to disengage the aged man from his speech.

Without hesitation Dean immediately walks off of the elevator as the doors open. Flabbergasted, the old man is frozen still. The lack of movement by his companion registers with Dean and he rotates around fully to see if everything is alright. The elderly man looks puzzled and jilted. Dean realizes that he wants to finish the conversation so he turns slightly to feign interest. It is not subtle enough and becomes obvious to both. There needs to be closure on the subject and it is offered by the more experienced of the two.

"Oh, I'm good."

The closure is weak and they both know that it is weak. Dean yells as he saunters away from the figure towards the parking lot.

"Well good for you."

The sun forces Dean to squint his eyes, possibly on purpose, as he walks out of the main doors. The celestial body has been around for long enough to see much good and much evil in the world. It has almost completed the day's descent from overhead.

After his eyes adjust to the light Dean straightens his posture and walks to the north-east corner. Waiting patiently for the light to turn green he makes his way across the street towards the lot containing his car and the cars of many of the workers in his building. The traffic is just starting to get busy but the streets are still safe to cross.

While walking across the street Dean is careful enough to stay within the boundaries of the two parallel, white lines. Once across, he spins again and walks into the parking lot. It is directly across from his building, but without fail, Dean crosses only at the corner. He moves to the very end of the first row where he parked his car earlier this morning.

His car is not the most expensive in the lot nor is it the least expensive. It is a heavy, dark blue conservative model of a fairly recent year. The finish is nicely waxed and the insides are immaculate. The white trim on the tires are still clean and complete.

Dean feels his pant pockets for his keys. He cannot feel the edgy bulge indicative of a set of keys and therefore reaches his free hand into the inner pocket of his suit jacket. Pulling them out, he fiddles with the keys until he can situate the one for the car between the thumb and forefinger of his hand.

Dean unlocks the door. Opening the driver door first he wraps his arm around to the back and pulls the knob to unlock the back door. His distorted reflection stares at him from the back window while he lifts the lever to gain access to the back seat where he places his briefcase. Then he takes off his jacket and lays it carefully on top. He climbs into the driver side of the car after firmly shutting the back door.

Sitting comfortably in a driving position he adjusts the three mirrors- the rear view mirror, the left side view and the right side view mirrors. Though they end up in the exact same position in which they started his mind can only rest if they are corrected before he starts the vehicle.

The key slides into the ignition. Dean pumps the gas peddle once before turning the key to initiate the spark. The charge strikes the fuel with precision. The motor sounds clean. Idling a fraction too high for Dean, he pumps the gas again. The act simply clears the gas line of excess fuel and the motor softens to a purr.

To fill the car with a more melodic noise Dean turns on the radio. A nice, soft volume level echoes off of the interior and he again tries to crack his neck without success.

Checking over both of his shoulders before anything else he puts the car into reverse and backs up out of the space. The car is long, so Dean backs straight out for more than half of the length of the car before turning the wheels. He moves from reverse into drive without applying the breaks and slowly rolls out towards the street.

He verifies movement in both directions, for potential dangers, before indicating his turn. Only then does he come to a complete resting position. Since the stop light at which he crossed is stale red Dean pulls out of the parking lot turning right. His drive home usually only takes about forty-five minutes but with the lighter traffic today he may make it even faster.

Dean does not usually listen to the music on the radio. He never drives without the radio on, and the station is always tuned appropriate to his choice at the time but the radio is something to which he does not listen. The music has to be loud enough for him to hear but is never so loud that it would catch his interest. It can be likened to the ambiance music that accompanies a glass of white wine in front of a café in Paris, France. Music, like the sounds of passing motorists or quiet philosophical chats, that are a necessity given the location but which would be overlooked in the description while one tells of a story. The music should never break his concentration.

What he is concentrating on instead is certainly not driving. Dean is not an exceptional driver. He is, in fact, much worse than the average person. Dean is also the perfect example of a person who can be so courteous and kind in regular activities but who loses all of his endearing qualities when behind the wheel.

In addition to his bad habit of never signalling, Dean swerves incessantly. The two bad habits may not be mutually exclusive conditions. The appearance that he may give to an outside observer while he changes lanes is that he has fallen asleep at the wheel.

The properly executed lane change is a three step process. The first step is to communicate a desired change to the other motorists by signalling with the direction indicator. The key here is to remain on a straight path or a path that is consistent with the contours of the road being travelled. Next, for safety concerns, is a check over the shoulder of the changing motorist to ensure that all other motorists are aware of the movement and that no automobile is hidden unaware in close proximity. Finally, there is a graceful glide from one lane into the other to complete the transaction.

The initial problem with Dean is that he regularly veers from one side of the lane to the other. He is pretty consistent in that he rarely crosses into another lane, though the perception is that he will. The movement is not a slow shift. They are sharp, quick movements.

The other main contributor to Dean's bad driving is that he drives out of habit. There is never a process of decision making during an extended trip. At times, Dean will travel through a traffic light without even glancing at the colour. He follows the other motorists but does not necessarily make decisions himself.

When changing lanes, the impression is that Dean inadvertently swerved too far beyond the lines to turn back. Rather than face the discomfiture with the other drivers he makes it look intentional. There would not have been an indicating signal nor would the glide be graceful. Dean would have zipped across his lane at a high pace, stopped briefly at the hashed white line, then zipped farther into the new lane without cause for concern. Without cause for *his* concern anyway.

More aggravating still is that Dean does not even like to change lanes. He much prefers sitting in the passing lane regardless of the amount of traffic and without consideration of the speed limit. The fact of the matter is that the left lane is not reserved for speedy motorists. The theory of the left lane is to ensure an open lane for passing.

Theoretically, all modern freeways need only be two lanes wide in each direction. The wider freeways are traditionally used to ease excessive congestion in major cities. Two lanes should always be enough, in theory. The idea is that all automobiles would travel in the right lane. If one were to approached an automobile travelling at a slower rate than desired then the motorist could pass on the left. There would be no congestion because all motorists could travel at their own speed without being stuck behind a slower moving automobile for more time than required to pass on the left.

Dean, and all people like Dean, destroys the theory in practice. By clogging the designated passing lane they prohibit other motorists from travelling at their own desired speed. The only motorist who can remain in the designated passing lane without destroying the theory is the motorist who is travelling faster than any other automobile on the road.

In Dean's opinion, time is money. There is never enough time. He needs to get anywhere that he is going in a hurry. This does not mean that Dean increases his speed. That would be illegal. The illusion is that by travelling in the passing lane, incorrectly known as the fast lane, Dean will arrive at any destination quicker.

There is a brief moment, while one is sitting on a stationary train, where he or she will have the impression that they are travelling backwards. It happens when another train looks stationary but is moving in the opposite direction. It is an illusion caused by relative motion. It is the same relative motion that gives the appearance that Dean is parked while driving in the passing lane of his freeway.

Checking his blind spot is a routine avoided as frequently as the proverbial electrician pulling up his pants. It is another prospect that could possibly make Dean an anecdote in the life of a cohort cruising along the freeway. Fortunately, he would never be aware of the anecdote. Dean never notices disgruntled drivers. His perfectly angled rear view mirror gets as much attention as traditional holiday fruitcake in July.

The most probable option about what captivates Dean's mind while driving is that he is trying to come up with more ways for criminals to beat the legal system. Dean does not now have, nor has he ever had the courage to boldly break the laws that he altruistically up holds. He does however enjoy using his unimaginative mind to create methods that *he* would employ to break the law should the need ever arise.

It is unfathomable how someone can work so frequently and intimately with the criminal mind yet be so naive as to the dark side of the law. The ghosts of intellect and imagination are not necessarily borne of noble descendants.

When Dean was about seventeen years old he got into a fight with one of the Romano twins. The catalyst for the fight is long forgotten but does not matter greatly anyway. Dean was battered quite badly and did not heal for some time. It was not a long bout and finished when the assaulting Romano stood up to leave. Dean was not aware that the twins were set to depart and still feared for more torment. As the idle brother turned his back Dean threw a rock in his direction. Dean does not have good aim and was not attempting any cavalier defence. The rock hit the head of the passive Romano knocking him to the ground with a thud. The retaliation unnerved the once aggressive twin enough to render him frozen.

Dean jumped to his feet. His adrenalin started pumping in his arteries. Not knowing the proper etiquette for a formal retaliation, Dean acted on the first impulse that formed in his cranium. He ran over to the kid and started punching.

Ironically, it scared Dean for weeks. He had never thought himself capable of such violence. He never really wanted to be capable of such violence. The thought of the police coming to his house did not give him much rest either. Even at *that* time, Dean wanted to be fully prepared.

He wondered about what he would say when the judge asked him about his defence. Why did he do it? What was his reasoning? Had Dean learned his lesson?

Though his mindset at the time of the assault was for his own protection, he could not claim self-defence. It simply would not hold on the cross examination. Dean had knocked the kid into a coma or at the very least unconscious. What danger does a comatose body represent? How would he explain as an impulse the actions of getting up off of the ground to move closer to the limp body then squatting on the chest of a boy who was not the initial aggressor and punching him several times about the face?

For months Dean worked on his speech but nothing was amassing. It was about that time when Dean first stumbled onto alcohol.

The discovery came less than six months after the incident when Dean and a few of his friends found some beer in the park. They decided to experiment by consuming the bottles in the woods on the south side of the gardens.

It was in a drunken stupor that Dean finally faced the judge who had been haunting him for so long. The scene, vivid in Dean's head, was acted for the amusement of his friends. The judge asked for Dean's explanation so he stood up straight. He masked his scared seventeen year old face with the face of a hardened criminal. It was Dean's impersonation of a soul beaten, hardcore, tough guy who coyly pretended to be rehabilitated.

His friends of course saw something different. They recognized an historically conservative boy grossly inebriated from four condition chilled beers acting like a madman.

Dean revolved as though addressing the twelve members of the jury and calmly spoke.

"Please listen your honour, members of the jury. You have got me all wrong. I didn't mean to beat him senseless. To me, it was all in good fun."

Dean laughed as his friends joined in on the fun protesting his illegitimate argument with sighs of disbelief and wailing their arms frantically.

"All in good fun? You threw a rock at him."

Dean had to calm them before continuing. There was too much interference in his head. The validity of existence is not in life but is in thought. Again addressing the players from the act within his head he rebutted the argument.

"But your honour, I didn't mean to hit him."

In the entire time that Dean had been imagining his own defence, *this* issue was never resolved to satisfaction. There is a condition for which Dean was striving.

Performances on television and in movies rely on testimony as dramatically as the legal system. Critically acclaimed scenes and recitals have been noted through their precision in execution. The flawless deliveries of poignant words at a crucial moment become flags for generations of people to wave. Dean strived to create such a moment with his testimony.

The tossing of the rock could be dismissed as self-defence. The issue had always been about the aggression after the boy lay unconscious. To achieve the flawless delivery Dean had to speak uninterrupted and eloquently. He started again from the beginning.

"But your honour, I did not mean to hit him. I am, I fear, a victim of circumstance. After I threw the rock, your honour, I will admit that I was quite petrified. I did not know how serious the wound was and I still remembered that I was outnumbered. The fact remains that the brother who started beating me in the first place was still conscious and perhaps even more angered by my retaliation.

"It was then, your honour, that I heard the horns of a fleet of automobiles. It was a spectacle like no other before it and one whose true magnificence would be weakened by words alone. A glorious fleet of automobiles from a visiting convention for German engineered cars happened to be passing by.

"If it pleases the court, I will suggest that I had no choice in the matter. The only people within the large radius of land were the three of us, and yet there were so many cars. Punch buggy black, punch buggy blue, punch buggy red…"

There was a roar from the gallery in the courtroom of Dean's mind. The gavel of the judge was pounded for silence but the victory was all but delivered. Case closed on the punch buggy assault.

Dean is almost halfway through his drive home and he is still in one piece. All of his attention and strain is in deep concentration of the automobile directly in front of him. Dean is staring like a watchful cat perched on top of a neighbouring fence. He becomes oblivious to almost everything else around him. Like a fading screen his peripheral vision disappears.

The car in front of him has a license plate that reads, "IEM 165".

In all likelihood Dean is intently working through the details of the license plate. It is another example of Dean's inability to define true crime and his quest for fooling the judicial system.

It is the type of license plate that Dean has wanted to purchase for a number of years.

The first time that Dean received a speeding ticket, he was more interested in what the police officer did when he returned to the cruiser with Dean's license and ownership than he was in the cost of the ticket. He wanted to know for what the fancy computer attached to the dash board was being used. It made sense that Dean would be queried in the computer system to see if he had any outstanding warrants for his arrest or unpaid parking tickets. There was probably a way to ensure that the car belonged to him as well. There were details about the search however that Dean needed to understand.

He wanted to know if the officer would run all license plates in the same fashion. Would it make a difference, for example, if the plates were not local? Would vanity license plates need to be checked separately? It is difficult for Dean to imagine that every possible combination of letters and numbers for any license plate across the continent could be referenced on a single database. This was his concern the first time that he received a speeding ticket.

If Dean is correct and both the type and location of a plate determines which database an officer accesses when verifying information, is it not possible that a terrible person could escape custody simply because an officer searches through the wrong system? Dean could purchase a personalized license plate that looks incredibly similar to a regular license plate and could race around town knocking down old people without getting charged with manslaughter.

The difficulty is not in the logic. The difficulty is instead in justifying his choice of letters and numbers. Dean would of course never engage in such activity but it is again a probability of thoughts that may be the focal point of his imagination while driving home. It is a game that he plays to pass time.

In reference again to the car in front of him, an argument could be made that the driver simply weighs one hundred and sixty-five pounds. It is likely that Dean's search for the ideal criminal vanity plate would not end here for a reason as equally ridiculous. There is nothing to differentiate body weight from possible age. A similar plate may result in a routine traffic stop to ensure that the one hundred sixty five year old driver has all of his or her papers in order. The legal system remains intact.

Time passes without acknowledgement and once Dean exits the highway a battle against time commences. He becomes overwhelmed with a need to go to the washroom. He does not torture himself by recalling his decision to leave behind the toilet on the ground floor of his office building. There is no reason for Dean to revisit the past.

The remaining distance to his home seems to stretch in length. Worse still is his fortune for timing the stop lights. Not only does he need to stop for each one but the duration is certainly extended for his discomfort alone. His free leg takes to activity and shakes to assist in the battle against his bladder.

It is going to be a tight race. Though hesitant on potentially endangering the lives of the people in his neighbourhood Dean has to increase his speed. In addition to driving faster he positions his car closer to each of the inside curbs while taking corners. The distance that this type of manoeuvre would save for such a short drive is minimal but gives the perception of cutting time.

There are signs posted along major freeways that detail the distance from any point along the route to designated destinations. It is used to inform those travellers who are less familiar with local geography. Dean has wondered on many long trips about the posted distances. From where is the distance measured? His initial belief was that the distance was an estimate of the gap in standard units of measure between the posted sign and the outskirts of the city or town in question. To keep his mind occupied he has monitored the accuracy of the postings on longer trips and has noticed something peculiar.

The average distance seems to be more accurate over longer gaps than is the accuracy for shorter drives. This confusion lead Dean to hypothesize that the posted distance is measured not from the outskirts of the town or city, but by a more central location. Perhaps the distances would be measured from the town or city hall.

The inexact measurement over longer drives has also been the centre of attention for Dean in another way. Rather than fight traffic, Dean likes to travel during very early mornings when covering larger distances. This of course means that fewer people are on the road.

Dean uses his understanding that while rounding a bend the outside lane is forced to travel a slightly longer distance. Though Dean could switch lanes anyway, it is still safer to switch repeatedly with fewer cars on the road. This is especially true for Dean.

There was a time when he was researching a case and drove a long way to a neighbouring city on a regular basis. On the days when he could travel in the early hours of morning he would switch lanes to ensure that each corner was taken from the inside lane to see if the measured distance would dramatically fall. The distance travelled did fall but there was nothing at all dramatic about the amount.

Dean is forced to hum as well in the losing battle against his bladder. There is a sharp pain beginning to form in his stomach. The effectiveness of his shaking leg is waning but Dean supports his leg's protest by rocking his upper body it the seat.

Another victim caught helplessly in the clutches of an insomniac's dementia.

Both the rocking of his torso and the shaking of his leg stops abruptly and Dean squeezes his legs together in a final effort as he glides onto his driveway and into the garage. As the garage door lowers to the ground the light from inside becomes more evident. He shuts the car off before even gearing into park but cannot take out the key.

"Damn Swiss and their safety measures."

The people of Switzerland are not even responsible for the type of car that Dean is driving. They are merely the verbal victims of a man in obvious pain. They became the target primarily because they are regarded as industry leaders in safety measures for automobiles. They could be considered responsible indirectly because they would have raised the global standards.

Dean does not have the time to grab his personal belongings from the back seat. With an awkward gate he waddles up the short set of stairs in the garage to the entrance of his home that is off of the kitchen. He walks past the dining area and into the main entrance lobby where he would normally deposit his shoes. The main floor bathroom is just around the corner.

The muscles in the lower half of Dean's body are clenched so tightly that he very nearly convulses. In his haste, he forces the door shut behind him but fails to close it completely. The stale air from inside the house gathers to create too much drag. Dean does not bother closing it completely because he is aware that he is the only one at home.

Once relieved, Dean saunters with a gained ease of his motions to the living room downstairs in order for him to relax. He plops his body down on the couch and sighs. Remembering that he needs to revisit his car to collect his jacket and briefcase he sits forward but the motion does not deliver enough momentum to bring him to his feet. Shrugging his shoulders in response to his dilemma he becomes content with his silent decision of the procrastination of his task. Dean uses his right foot to ease off his left shoe then returns the favour by switching feet and leans back into the moulded cushions of the couch.

He can feel the force of gravity pulling at his body. It has been pulling at him all day but he takes special stock of it now. He cocks his head around in an attempt to locate something. His vantage point is ineffective which causes him to stand.

Dean leans over the edge of the couch and looks beneath the table beside it.   There are some magazines stacked meticulously underneath. He selects three from the middle section and disturbs the neat arrangement when pulling them out.

Back on the couch, he leafs through the first one until he finds an article that he has not yet read. The other two magazines are tossed onto the coffee table in front of him.

Dean picks up the remote control and turns on the television without looking. Like the music in his car, there needs to be a level of noise in the room to fill the void. He does not even choose a channel but engages in the article from the magazine.

About twenty minutes later Dean is startled by his wife. She appears from out of nowhere in the entrance to the living room. He has stopped reading the magazine, though it still lies in his lap. It would appear that he is watching television but he is not. Crossed one over the other, his feet are on top of the coffee table much to the dismay of his wife.

"Oh. Hello there. I didn't know you were home."

Immediately, Dean lowers his feet from the table. She walks over with her arm outstretched silently asking for something. Dean realizes that she is requesting the magazine from his lap.

"My goodness, you nearly scared me half to death."

She takes the magazine from him and gathers the other two from off of the coffee table. The wallet in her hand causes her some trouble as she tries to align the magazines into a uniform bundle so she places it temporarily on the arm of the couch. There is a facial distortion of disapproval as she notices the disarray of the magazine stack below.

"I didn't see your shoes in the hall and I thought that you simply forgot to lock the door this morning."

Dean did not enter through the front door on his arrival. He does not share this information with his wife. The story is not neglected to stop from getting in trouble for the insecurity of their home, but rather to limit the need for her to hear about his battle against time.

"No. I was finished work a little early today."

"Oh isn't that nice? Well how *was* your day?"

"Same old thing. I didn't have to do that court appearance though. I guess the other party settled out of court and dropped the charges."

To truly experience the full effect of this conversation you have to use your imagination. Dean's voice is currently monotone. Gravity has drawn from him the energy needed to speak with fervour.

If one were to close one's eyes and only listen to this couple, he or she would be reduced to insanity. They are two middle aged individuals who are discussing with each other the very same subjects that they have discussed each and every day of each and every year of their relationship. It is not that they want to ask the same questions everyday. Their generation is one that considers the questions to be of good form. They do still have interest in the other's life but they have both found out that asking questions is not the way to gain the more relevant information.

As uninteresting as it may be, the only way to truly evoke a correct feel for another's life is to be drawn into the mundane and boring aspects of it. When people discuss their days with someone they typically mention only the highlights. They point out only those events that stand out from other days. People discuss these topics because it makes for more interesting conversation and because of a lack of time. Dean and his wife have learned this over time and complete their daily ritual only because it is the right thing to do.

The older generations cling to the notion that dreaming inspires greatness. People are not supposed to hold onto all of their dreams. What one becomes is directly mirrored by those things for which one strives. It is, however, necessary to trim away the excess.

Dean and his wife are both tired of answering the regular questions as well. They do so because it is the polite thing to do when someone asks.

"Now which one dropped the charges?"

She truly does not remember. In reality, she is indifferent but because it is her husband's business she takes an interest.

"Oh yes, it was the case with the elderly gentleman whose dog kept relieving itself on the neighbour's lawn."

He has never told her about this particular case. There is of course no way for her to dispute the fact.

"Oh right, now I remember."

"Yes, well everything seemed to work out for them. By the way, how was your day?"

"It wasn't anything special. I did my regular stuff. You know."

"Did the two of you get a chance to go out for lunch?"

Earlier in the day she phoned Dean mentioning that her friend was in town and that they may be going out to lunch.

"Well she came by, but she said that she had to run a few errands. She may be giving me a call to see if we could meet for dinner instead. Tomorrow, perhaps."

"Oh, it is too bad that you did not get together today but perhaps it will work out for tomorrow."

"Yes."

That is it. The two have completed their duties and life can again continue. The evening passes at a consistent rate and the two simply relax in the manor to which they have become accustomed. He briefs himself on upcoming court appearances in front of the television and she cooks dinner for them while listening to the radio and cleaning.

They eat their dinner in silence. It would be considered by nobody an awkward hush but a polite hush. It has none of the typical traits of a Hollywood silence that is filled with scraping plates and clanging utensils- a gap that is used to denote the idle passing of time before a new revelation. This is a real hush filled appropriately with soft, external distractions. There is the sound of a child playing outside or a motor turning over in the distance. Air can be heard blowing periodically through the vents.

It has not always been like this. They used to have interesting things to tell one another over dinner. Though, today is just an average day like the average days from years before. There is nothing that has happened that would be considered exciting. Nothing, that is, that has happened to them. This is not necessarily a negative situation.

Some people would declare that their silence is a testament of proper coupling. Two people fall in love and become so comfortable with each other that it is not necessary to talk all the time. There is a reason that silence is not for everyone.

Tonight, time is purely slipping past them. Day has quickly turned to night. Except for the requirement of turning on additional lights, the metamorphosis has transpired without their knowledge. A night such as this one is being wholly wasted on them. It is the masses of people like Dean and his wife who are insufficiently altruistic to step out of character and enjoy the little things.

Tonight the sky is turning *that* unusual colour. Like when a passionate sunset leaves the heavens a brilliant red with wrestling purple and violet hues. Except *this* is at night and the colour is black and not red. The sky tonight is a passionate black on black. The unusual sight is giving a complete feeling of tranquillity throughout.

Anyone who dare gaze at the sky for long enough tonight would succumb and would be overwhelmed by a peaceful feeling. It is as though everything in the world is just working out for one night. For perhaps the first time since the creation of the universe there is no disequilibrium. All of the tumblers in the metaphoric clock of life are reaching the end and tomorrow starts a brand new era.

It will only be a brand new era, however, for those who recognize the signs tonight. For Dean and his wife and the millions of people around the world who are exactly the same tomorrow is just another day.

It is difficult to say for certain what is right. It is essential to separate oneself from his or her current position to establish more clearly where one is. Stepping out of the present can be revealing. If you never step back to see where you are then you never get a chance to miss where you have been.

The night sky tonight is enchanting, dark as it may be.

As Dean prepares himself for bed his wife departs to shower. They do not discuss their individual plans as routine still dictates the night. He retrieves his pyjamas from a chair in the corner of the bedroom and slips them on with a rush. There is no open window from which to hide, nor any other person in the room. It is habitual for Dean to dress himself quickly when pulling up his pants.

After dressing for sleep he positions himself under the covers in bed and does nothing. His eyes only watch the ceiling because the ceiling is overhead. Dean can hear the water stop from the shower in the bathroom a dozen feet away. His eyes do not move.

The light exposed from both the area under the door and in the crack between the top of the door and the frame is extinguished before the door opens a few minutes later. Dean does not need to watch his wife as she collects her ensemble for tomorrow and sets it aside for easy access. His eyes blink for the needed moisture but remain on the ceiling as she sits on the edge of her side and fiddles with her alarm clock.

She reaches over and turns out the light on her night stand then crawls under the blanket. The beautiful night does not cloud them in darkness but leaves a soft glow with which they can still see. Her head softly hits the pillow and she lets out a soft sigh.

Dean finally turns to her as a grin helplessly crosses his face. There is a certain comfort that he feels from her warm body but the emotion is authentic and originates from his love. He can vaguely make out the lines of her face in the dark, but it would not matter. He can picture everything about her.

Dean turns again and lifts his head to rework his pillow. The admirable couple lay frozen by time. The sounds around them cease before she speaks.

"I love you."

The sentiment catches Dean by surprise despite the fact that it should not. The usual response is to restate the same. Dean has not given the usual response for years because it seems for him to be expected. There is another sentiment that he has adopted. He knows that his wife is being genuine and that she is not seeking comfort in idle flattery. She is in fact not expecting a response at all.

"You are the most important thing in my life."

She turns to see his face but he is again gazing at the ceiling and does not meet her. Wiggling her head to get comfortable for a second time she whispers her final words for the night.

"Goodnight Dean."

Dean breathes deeply with his eyes now closed. Another valuable second of the atypical night slowly passes before he responds.

"Goodnight Elinore."

It seems that people are always searching for the great explanation that will clarify exactly what it is that brings them together with everyone else in the world. It is less important to express that which brings people together than it is to illustrate that which does not set them apart. Therefore, the solution to the question can be found not in the answers that people provide but in the effortless act of asking. The explanation will forever remain incomplete.

Printed in the United States
818100003B

9 781403 355515